Thoughts about Make Rain by Other Rainmakers

"If you are a Rainmaker, or wish t
Jeffrey J. Fox, Author

"This book fills a gap in the crowde
very different from all the other boo... and in many ways it is also
much better. *Make Rain* is a collection of short one and a half page
inspirational messages. Each message can stand alone, so the reader
will get value already after the first couple of pages. The value of the
book simply accumulates as you turn each page. No other book in
my library of books on sales can make such a claim! *Make Rain* is a
great book to have with you everywhere. You can use any break in
the day to consume a message or two, but do yourself a favour and
think carefully about the messages you read. Each of the messages
actually has the potential to change your life – for the better."
Hans Peter Bech, Author of the Amazon #1 bestseller
Building Successful Partner Channels.

"Brilliant! *Make Rain* is a must read for sales professionals,
sales managers and entrepreneurs who are looking to challenge
themselves to a new standard. It's the conversational, easy to read
storytelling with real world examples that keeps you hooked. I
certainly was."
Steve Claydon - Author of the #1 bestseller,
THE DIARY OF A S.U.C.C.E.S.S. DRIVEN KID,
thought leading Sales Trainer, Serial entrepreneur.

"A book like this, jam-packed with precious facts, pragmatic steps
and practical wisdom, does not get written very often."
Derin Cag, CEO and Founder of Richtopia.

"Engaging! Daily affirmations for those sales people who desire
to really stand out. Ideas, challenges, and inquisitive thought that
drives any burgeoning sales person to keep reading!"
Matt Lane, President, DCIM Division, Geist Global.

"The sales person and indeed the nature of selling is changing, requiring new ways of thinking and performing. The great thing about *Make Rain* is that anyone can read it and put the author's thoughts and ideas into practice right away. Is the Rainmaker the new salesperson? Quite possibly."

Janice B. Gordon, Visiting Fellow, Cranfield School of Management and Author of *Business Evolution: Creating Growth in a Rapidly Changing World.*

"Many of the insights in *Make Rain* seem to come at you left field, challenging the status quo of how you think about selling and sales. I recommend everyone who wants to achieve results read this book"

Brian Burns, Co-author of *Selling in a New Market Space* and Host of *The Brutal Truth about Sales & Selling Podcast.*

Make Rain, is a wonderful piece of business non-fiction. It is elegantly yet humbly written. It's almost like Jonas is having a quiet one-on-one conversation with you, challenging you to think before you act!

Jack Mizel, CEO, Institute of Sales Management. (From the foreword)

MAKE RAIN

Dear Emeka,

May the content of this
book inspire you to be
the best version of yourself.
God Bless,

[signature]

MAKE RAIN

180 Powerful Insights into How Rainmakers
Sell Their Way to Financial Success

Jonas Caino

Rainmethods Media & Publishing

Published by Rainmethods Media & Publishing
Sheriffs Orchard,
Coventry, CV1 3PP
Tel: +44 (0) 121 6999001
Website: www.rainmethods.com
Email: publisher@rainmethods.com

First published in Great Britain in 2016

ISBN: 978-0-9954836-0-6 (Paperback)
        978-0-9954836-1-3 (Kindle)
        978-0-9954836-2-0 (Hardcover)

British Library Cataloguing-in-Publication Data
A catalogue record for this book is available from the British Library

The publisher's policy is to use paper manufactured from sustainable forests.

To the love of my life, my eternal flame, my best friend.

Table of Contents

Part Two   The Rainmaker's Practice

Acknowledgements

As I write these acknowledgements, the old saying "no one can sing a symphony" springs to mind. This book would not have been possible if not for the intellect, patience, focus and sheer brilliance of some wonderful individuals. Here we go.

To...

All my mentors, past and present, physical and virtual. What you've all shared is real and has shaped the professional I am.

The team at Rainmethods Media & Publishing: the world beckons.

Marek Stuczynski: your attention to detail is actually scary. You the Man.

James Millington: editor extraordinaire. Cheers Mate.

To Hope: without you, excellence, learning and boldness would not be my watchwords. Thanks Mum.

To "the Man who brought back the Crown Jewels". Thanks Dad.

To my siblings, Andy, Richard & (Dr) Tina: your support has been massive.

To my little Rainmakers, Jojo and Benji: a father's love for his sons knows no bounds.

To Serina, my love, my rock, my all: thanks for holding on with love, encouragement and positivity.

Finally, nothing would ever be possible without God. Thank you Lord.

"I cannot teach anybody anything;
I can only make them think".
Socrates.

Foreword

Buying and selling have always been and will continue to be the cornerstones of economic progress. For 30 years, selling has been a profession and a passion for me. In my opinion, we should all view the ability to sell solutions, concepts, ideas and indeed yourself as a critical life skill for anyone and everyone. Deep down I believe that there are three "pillars" that are foundational to success in selling. The first is knowledge: knowledge of yourself, your profession, your goals and how they are executed to arrive at the desired outcome. The second is presentation: how to develop relationships and manage yourself and others. Finally, commitment: being able to gain the commitment for what you want from others, which makes everything come together.

Imagine, therefore, my surprise when Jonas (who, I might add, has been a Fellow of our illustrious Institute for a number of years) finally caught up with me after some persistence, pitched his project and sent me the *Make Rain* manuscript. All my thoughts about selling flowed within those pages. I simply couldn't put the manuscript down. I telephoned him and I found that his thoughts on selling and on transcending rainmaking skills to people from all walks of life were eerily similar to mine. So when he asked me to write this foreword, I was delighted to accept.

Make Rain is a wonderful piece of business non-fiction. It is elegantly yet humbly written. It's almost like Jonas is having a quiet one-on-one conversation with you, challenging you to think before you act! I'm making a bold statement in saying that *Make Rain* is for *everyone*. If you are new to selling, start with this book. If you're an "old hat" like me, you can gain new perspectives with this book. If you are a business owner, absorb this book and if you simply want to get more out of life and personal relationships then enjoy this book. And see just how far rainmaking can take you.

Jack Mizel,
CEO, Institute of Sales Management.

Prologue

What Have You Achieved Today?

I'm a salesman. No really, I am. I'm not a sales guru, a trainer or a consultant, nor am I someone who paints pretty pictures about the art and science of selling and hands out prescriptions on how to sell and influence people. Nope. I'm a regular salesperson just like you. I have a boss and he has a boss. Like you, I have to deal with the pain and pleasure of hunting for business, global conference calls at six in the morning and eleven at night, difficult emails from irate customers, the sick feeling before you go in to negotiate the deal of your life, managing the difference between forecasting and soothsaying, dealing with different personalities and still trying to remember yours. Oh, yes, I'm a salesman…and I love what I do.

A few years ago, I managed a small team of salespeople. They were all young, eager and inexperienced. They came from a variety of backgrounds. My aim with this team was to develop them into successful sales professionals, into true Rainmakers. I organised sales training seminars that increased the team's output for a period of about two weeks. However they would then go back into their old ways of the usual habits such as only dealing with prospects and customers they were comfortable with, vague and sloppy forecasting, not paying attention to key details, forgetting to follow up on agreed customer actions in a timely fashion, asking the wrong questions in the wrong way, just focusing on our offering and not on the customers' business…the list would go on.

So I had a thought. Coaching! Maybe, the slow feeding of skills and practice could change their behaviour over time. Good idea, but the problem was that both I and my team didn't have the time for regular, detailed, one-on-one coaching.

One day, whilst driving and listening to the BBC on the radio, the *Thought for the Day* bulletin programme came on air. This is a three- to four-minute daily broadcast about an idea, a thought, a concept, an insight that is designed to challenge the listener and make them stop and think. Eureka! A light bulb came on. "Why don't I provide my team with a thought for the day to supplement the training and some one-on-one coaching sessions?" I asked myself. So I embarked on daily "virtual coaching" sessions.

Every morning at 6 am I would fire up my laptop and spend half an hour or so writing an "insight" and then email the team. I entitled the daily email with a challenge: *"What Have You Achieved Today?"* I encouraged my team to digest these snippets and put them into practice *in their own way*. I did this for nine months without fail.

The impact was immediate and far-reaching. Their pipelines started to increase dramatically, their revenue followed suit and so did profit margins. I was doing my job and it showed. Most importantly though, the team transformed their own lives and bank balances. The curious thing was that by the time I stopped, over 100 salespeople had somehow found their way onto the email chain and were demanding more.

Many people have urged me to share these insights with a wider audience. I was reluctant at first as I felt this whole writing thing would be a distraction from my job. But someone said something that made me change my mind. *"If you have a message, why deny the world of it?"* So I heeded the advice and lo and behold, here we are.

Make Rain is for professional salespeople. Whether you are new to selling and need some direction or you're a "veteran" looking for a nudge, *Make Rain* is easy to read and digest, yet packed full of inspiring ideas. Curiously, entrepreneurs and professionals (lawyers, accountants and consultants) will also benefit hugely from reading this book. It's not written to be prescriptive. It won't *teach* you line by line how to sell and influence people—there are thousands of sales books that can do that for you. This book is designed to make you think about what you are doing daily: your thoughts, habits and behaviour. It challenges you to make the changes necessary to be a successful Rainmaker. The presupposition here is that you are the master of your destiny and that you are unique. So it's up to you to develop or adapt the habits needed to be successful. This book will help point you in the right direction.

Abraham Lincoln once stated, "Give me six hours to chop down a tree and I will spend the first four sharpening the axe". I believe before one can excel, one has to *prepare* to excel. With that in mind, *Make Rain* is written in two parts. The first part focuses on the mind-set of the Rainmaker. This section challenges as well as encourages you to focus on your existing attitudes and outlook. The second part deals with the ideas, techniques and skills Rainmakers use to be successful.

You can read this book from cover to cover in three hours or so, read an insight a day, or simply browse through it from time to time (recommended) until an insight hits you like a lightning bolt and compels you to act! It's entirely your choice.

I hope you enjoy reading this book as much as I have enjoyed writing it and that it will have an impact on your professional life in some way.

Part One

The Rainmaker's Mindset

"The key is not the will to win... everybody has that.
It is the will to prepare to win that is important".

Bobby Knight

Insight I

The Rainmaker

The Native American tribes used Rainmakers to protect their harvest. Rainmakers would perform dances and other rituals to *communicate, influence and negotiate* with the gods to make it rain. At the time, this was seen as the most important job anyone could do. Why? Because the livelihood and indeed the lives of communities literally depended on rain, particularly during periods of severe drought. These *special* individuals were highly respected and revered in their communities. They also spent their entire lives developing their craft and honing their skills in order to produce the results necessary for the survival of their people. In hindsight, *Rainmakers* of old were probably just very good at reading and following meteorological patterns and the rest may have simply been smoke and mirrors. Nevertheless, pseudo-scientific skills were still required to achieve this.

There are strong parallels we can draw from the Rainmaking of Native Americans and Rainmaking today. Organisations, be they businesses, charities and government institutions all need customers and their money to achieve their goals. These goals could include growth, market share, increased shareholder value, return on investment or even altruistic goals.

Since the dawn of industrialisation and the beginnings of a dedicated organisational sales force, there has always been an individual or a small group of people within the sales force who were deemed "special". These people, for some reason, seemed to bring in most of the business for the company they worked for. Over time these "special ones" became known as Rainmakers. They didn't necessarily have to be salespeople, they could be lawyers, entrepreneurs, accountants or investment bankers who just brought in more clients to the firm than any other. In the 1980s, interested people like Neil Rackham, Michael Bosworth, Robert Miller and Stephen Heiman studied what Rainmakers did differently from others. This research, by them and many more since, now makes it possible for others to *learn and model* the skills and mind-set Rainmakers possess and to create similar results.

The reality is simple. *Anyone* can become a Rainmaker and become fabulously wealthy. You just have to *want* to be one; I mean really want to become one. Then you must be *committed* to being one. And then you have to go through the gruelling (but ultimately rewarding) process of *learning, studying and modelling* to be one with a discipline and dedication you never knew you could muster. By never giving up, one day, your bank balance and the state of your life will tell you that you are a Rainmaker.

> Remember: Being a Rainmaker, like success, is a binary choice— to become or not to become.

Insight 2

Are You Sure This is What you Want to Do?

"The wealthiest places in the world are not gold mines, oil fields, diamond mines or banks. The wealthiest place is the cemetery. There lie companies that were never started, masterpieces that were never painted...In the cemetery there is buried the greatest treasure of untapped potential. There is a treasure within you that must come out. Don't go to the grave with your treasure still within YOU".

This quotation by the late Dr Myles Munroe, OBE, struck a chord with me. What is the point of life and in living if you can't discover and fulfil your God-given potential?

I believe this is the starting point of becoming a Rainmaker. If you are striving to become something you were not designed to be, you will always struggle with internal misalignment.

The good news is that any personality type can become a Rainmaker. Anyone can excel at selling. However, getting to the top of your game (any game) and staying there requires vision, focus, determination, boldness, humility, inner strength and openness. You cannot attain this if your life's work is one hard demoralising slog.

For years, my advice to newcomers to the selling game has often been to search deeply and honestly and resolve in your mind what you want to do and who you want to become.

I always get the question back: "How do I know what I am

destined to become?" The short answer is that you don't, well not for sure anyway. The long answer is that you can get a *sense of direction* by simply asking yourself, "If I had all the resources I needed, what would I want to do, who would I become?" The answer to this litmus question will at least give you a confident direction to begin your journey towards fulfilment.

Wherever that journey leads you to, be it a painter, a lawyer, a politician, an accountant, a musician or a salesperson; if you stride into your destiny confidently and purposefully, you'll end up being the Rainmaker in your space.

Remember: Your purpose in life is to find your life's purpose and dedicate your whole life to it.

Insight 3

For Lack of a Better Word...

"Greed is good!" Everyone remembers the words of Gordon Gekko from Oliver Stone's 1987 film, *Wall Street*. Opinions of that phrase have been polarised to this day. Many people will say that the phrase epitomises the primitive, excessive attitudes of the few, which creates a force that is so malignant, so destructive that it threatens our very way of life, our planet. This may be so when it comes to short-termism and the use of unethical methods to achieve entirely narrow-minded and unsustainable goals.

Consider, however, the actual context of Gordon Gekko's speech: "The point is, ladies and gentleman, that greed—for lack of a better word—is good. Greed is right. Greed works. Greed clarifies, cuts through, and captures the essence of the evolutionary spirit. Greed, in all of its forms—greed for life, for money, for love, knowledge—has marked the upward surge of mankind".

Greed, in this context, smacks of aspiration, ambition, the desire to be better, to push the boundaries of what's possible, to strive earnestly for excellence, to create and provide value; long term sustainable value, and to enjoy all the rewards—be they finances, personal satisfaction or security—that achievements bring.

Rainmakers know they exist not to be mere observers of progress but to be creators of profit for organisations. Profit creates jobs, social mobility and stability. Profit creates economic progress.

You are at the cutting edge of this process: the sharp end. In order to be successful in your endeavour, you *have* to want it, to really want it. You have to be *greedy* for progress, greedy for over-shooting targets, greedy for providing value to clients, greedy for achievement, greedy for passion, greedy for success, greedy for life. It's the lack of a better word that makes greed good.

Greed is only however the beginning of the achievement process. With greed comes hard work, dedication, focus, long term planning, preparation, courage, managing emotions, managing time, managing others, reciprocity, learning and self-mastery. It starts with greed and ends with accomplishment.

> # Remember: You have to want it—with every fibre in your being—to achieve it.

Insight 4

What Inspires You?

Seriously, what really inspires you? Only inspiration can motivate you. Only inspiration can keep you focussed over the long term. If you take the time to look into the lives of Rainmakers in various industries from all walks of life, every single one of them will say that what kept them striving towards their goal was something that *really inspired* them. They'll tell you that no matter how long it took or how hard the going got, inspiration was like an anchor, *a rock* that kept them planted and kept their eyes firmly fixed on the prize!

So, I'll ask again, what inspires you? A role model, an idea, a dream, an agreement, the past, God?

If nothing inspires you, then how can you have the *burning desire* to consistently achieve your goals, your team's goals, your company's goals? How can you have the conviction to see it through amongst all the competition, political insensitivities and stresses that comes with achieving?

You MUST be inspired. You have no choice. Look for your inspiration and when you find it, keep it burning bright and this will spur you on to achieve greatness in everything you do.

Remember: A small
seed of inspiration can
grow to a huge forest of
achievement!

Insight 5

Seeking Success or Avoiding Failure

Selling is a lonely job. Yes you might be part of a team, and yes you might have the support of an organisation behind you, but when all is said and done, the accounts are your responsibility, the number is yours to hit and no one else's. We all know it can get lonely out there.

Rainmakers however stay motivated. Irrespective of what is happening around them, they possess a highly developed way of staying clear on and certain of their goals all day, every day. They know that motivation is the burning coal that keeps the steam locomotive engine moving and if the coal stops burning it's game over—the party stops.

How do Rainmakers keep motivated? The answer is different for every Rainmaker out there, but one thing is clear: Rainmakers do not use gimmicky self-motivation techniques such as chanting affirmations all day long. Instead they ask themselves deep and relevant questions about why they do what they do and what outcomes they desire.

I recently watched a TEDx talk themed *Beyond Boundaries* by the Alumni Distinguished Professor at Virginia Tech, E. Scott Geller.

Geller posits that research shows that the key to self-motivation lies in seeking the answers to three powerful questions. So think about the desired goal at hand and ask yourself these questions:

Can I do it? Do you genuinely believe the goal can be achieved? Are you capable of doing it?

Will it work? Can you honestly state the goal is attainable if you do the right things? Do you have evidence that this can be done and has been done before?

Is it worth it? After all the risk, sweat, tears, late nights, early mornings, endless trips, disappointments, pain, strain on personal relationships, mistakes, setbacks, years of your life spent and then success...will it be worth it? Does the intended outcome align with expectations?

You will never be truly motivated if you can't answer these three questions positively. You will only find yourself in a state of avoiding failure, which is no foundation for high and consistent motivation. One must think deeply and honestly about these questions and seek positive answers to enter a state of seeking success. Do this today.

Remember:
Motivation is all about State.
Develop and stay in a success-seeking state and not in one that simply tries to avoid failure.

Insight 6

Rock Solid

A lot is known about Thomas J. Watson as the first president of IBM. The guy who turned the Computing Tabulating and Recording Company (CTR) into the global phenomenon we now know as IBM. Less is known about his days at National Cash Register (NCR). After going bust as a butcher in Buffalo, New York State and returning his leased cash register to NCR, Thomas Watson decided that he wanted to work for NCR as a salesman. The local sales manager at the time, John J. Range, didn't take Watson seriously and turned him down. Watson persisted and continued persisting until on a cold foggy day in November 1896, Range finally hired him as a sales apprentice. Initially Watson was a poor salesperson. But with Range's guidance and Watson's *rock solid commitment*, Watson was soon earning $100 commission a week (that's almost $3,000 a week in today's money).

The beginning, middle and end to all success is commitment. Rock Solid Commitment! The term "The Uncommitted Rainmaker" is an oxymoron. It doesn't exist. It's an impossibility. Without commitment, failure is assured.

To me, commitment starts with putting a stake in the ground and saying to yourself: "It starts right here! No going back! Whatever happens I will achieve this. I must achieve this". The interesting thing is that once you are committed, I mean really committed, things start to work out for you better than expected.

The question arises: *What are you really committed to?* Money, closing larger deals, smashing your targets, a better life, an amazing career? These are all worthy goals. But success comes and stays when one is committed to a higher ideal. Vince Lombardi, the great US football coach put it best: "The quality of a person's life is in direct proportion to their commitment to *excellence*, regardless of their chosen field of endeavour". To achieve all your goals, you must be committed to excellence. Excellence incorporates a lot of things: being better, sharper, more focussed, more professional, overcoming weaknesses, harnessing strengths, being positive, constant learning, adapting, practising, working well with others, understanding and appreciating yourself. Without excelling in areas like these you are wasting the world's time and your own, and success will always be on the distant horizon.

> # Remember: Stick to the deal you make with success and success will surely stick with you.

Insight 7

Hunger Struck!

One of the first things most sales managers and directors look for in a Rainmaker is the hunger for success. They know that without that overarching innate desire to succeed, all skills are ultimately rendered useless. One of the first questions I tend to ask at most sales job-related interviews I conduct is "Do you have a real hunger for succeeding here and if so, why?"

In Napoleon Hill's classic 1937 text *Think and Grow Rich*, Hill cites *desire* as the very first fundamental step towards creating wealth. Without a strong desire, need, passion, craving, urge, thirst, that deep hunger for success there will *be* no success. So what happens if due to pressure, challenges, moving goal posts, setbacks or even the initial taste of success, your motivation begins to fade? What happens when you become less hungry, in some cases quite full up or *fed* up? You need to get hungry again. If not, your slope gets slipperier by the month. You need to go on what I call the *Rainmaker's Diet*.

Rainmakers know that in order to be *and stay* successful, they have to be *and stay* hungry. Their desire has to be like a laser beam and if it's broken by distractions, it will never hit the intended target. To stay hungry you must simultaneously keep your mind in two extremes of your imagination. You must consistently go on two "Ebenezer Scrooge" journeys of the mind.

The first mental journey is pain-related. Take some time out and imagine that in today's environment of global and regional economic stagnation, you are no longer in employment and you have little hope of getting a job. You struggle to provide even the basics for you and your loved ones. Your mind is forever filled with money problems and as a result you feel like someone who will never taste even a hint success in this lifetime. Can you imagine how you would feel, how you would think, what your day-to-day existence would be like?

The second mental journey is pleasure-related. Again, take the time to vividly imagine you being at the top of your game. All debts paid off, with various savings and investments all ensuring that your mind is void of any money worries. You are living the kind of life you have always striven to live. You have more free time to do the things that can only enrich your life and those around you. You feel empowered, you feel like you are being who you were destined to be.

The power of the Rainmaker's Diet is the level of detail and vividness when you imagine these two scenarios. The more you crystallise every image in detailed colour, every feeling, every smell, every thought, every voice as real as possible during your two journeys, the more hungry you will end up becoming.

> # Remember:
> # In order to win, you must first feel like you've lost.

Insight 8

Who's in Charge Here?

The coming of age or rite of passage is a common concept in virtually all societies across the globe. It could be the *Seijin Shiki* of the Japanese or the *Bar Mitzvah* of Jewish law, or taking a journey on a *Vision Quest* as the Native Americans do; it could be as dangerous as teenage *male circumcision* performed in certain African cultures or as simple as just getting *married* or *graduating* from university.

Whatever the act, the theme remains the same: before coming of age, others were responsible for you; after the rites of passage, *you* are responsible for you. Setting aside the on-going philosophical debate over predestination versus free will, which belongs to the realms of esotericism, the real question is this: If you are not responsible for your life, your thoughts, your actions, your results, then who is? Life is about destiny and if someone has to steer the ship of your life, it might as well be you. Jim Rohn once stated, "You must take personal responsibility. You cannot change the circumstances, the seasons, or the wind, but you can change yourself. That is something you have charge of".

Rainmakers know intuitively that they are responsible for their actions and therefore the corresponding results. If they have setbacks, they don't look for others to blame, they swallow the bitter pill and learn from the experience for the *next time*. Conversely, with every win, large or small, personal or corporate, Rainmakers bask in the glory and enjoy the spoils.

Being responsible for your actions, even if someone else was actually performing them on your behalf, only serves to empower you. Blaming others only serves to sap you. Be responsible today and every day and you will personally benefit today and every day, and the good news is that you don't have to go through physically painful rites of passage to actually enjoy the benefits!

> # Remember:
> # It's up to you to do what it takes to get to where you need to be.

Insight 9

The Fake Half of Reality

In January 2007, American healthy lifestyle magazine *Prevention* published an article entitled *Go Ahead...Smile!* One of the interesting things the article stated was that in research at Wake Forest University, North Carolina, scientists asked a group of 50 students to *act* like extroverts for 15 minutes in a group discussion, even if they did not feel like it. The results were that the more assertive and energetic the students acted, the happier they became. These naturally introverted students had to *act as if* they were not introverts for a period.

I remember in the earlier years of my sales career having to go for an internal promotion interview as a senior sales associate, a job I felt was somewhat above my capabilities at the time. Nevertheless, I felt the role was a natural progression for me, but on looking at the job specification, I wasn't so sure any more. I discussed this with my mentor David. He intently examined the job specification sheet, looked up at me and said, "If you can do everything on this sheet well, then you are already over-qualified and the job is not for you. If, however, you can do only half of it, then you are well on your way to making an enjoyable success of it".

"What about the other half?" I asked, with a puzzled look on my face.

My mentor smiled and said, "Ah, yes. The other half...well you'll just have to fake it till you make it".

As a Rainmaker, one can never be content with any level of success. Whatever level you have achieved will always become a comfort zone. This comfort zone becomes the seed that ultimately causes the decline in one's figures and indeed one's career. The Rainmaker knows that to break into the next level of success, he or she has to first understand implicitly what is *required* to succeed at that level, access what strengths they already possess to achieve on that level and act as if they are *already* successful on that level.

Whatever and wherever you want and need to be, start today to fake it till you make it, then raise the bar and fake it again and again and one day you will be flabbergasted as to how far you've come.

> # Remember: Never stop using the power of imaginative desire to become.

Insight 10

Hear the Baseline

"Elementary, my dear Watson, elementary". Ah yes, the famous misquotation from Sir Arthur Conan Doyle's *Sherlock Holmes* novels. One can just imagine the pensive look on Holmes' face as he ponders over the simply impossible puzzle, only to dazzle Watson with his ingenious powers of deduction and therefore informing him yet again that it is all about the *basics*.

In reality, success is truly about getting the basics right. It is the deceptively simple process of doing the right things, in the right order, at the right time. This cuts through the over-complicated "stuff" that surrounds us in life and work.

A Rainmaker's strength is recognising what he needs to be good at and pouring all his time, effort, energy, commitment, passion and focus into all the activities that will achieve that goal. The Rainmaker's ultimate goal? To sell. They know that it is fundamental to stick to doing selling very well and not become distracted by other jobs, ideas, issues, politics and other diversions. These and many other things take one down alleys where there are no orders, no commission and far away targets.

Know the basics in selling such as Attention, Interest, Decision, Action (AIDA). Things like prospecting, qualifying, pre-closing, closing, adding value, service, building rapport, asking for referrals, knowing your customers and products inside out and being confident about your profession. These are some of the things to dwell on. Leave the rest to others.

> Remember: It's the elementary things done well that will lead you to Rainmaking success.

Insight II

View from the Hubble

In 1970, sociologist Dr. Edward Banfield of Harvard University wrote a book titled *The Unheavenly City*, in which he described one of the most profound sociological studies on successful versus unsuccessful people ever conducted.

Banfield's goal was to find out how and why some people became financially independent during the course of their working lifetimes and others didn't. He started off convinced that the answer would be found in factors such as their environment, family background, education, intelligence, influential contacts, or some other concrete factor. To Banfield's surprise, what he finally discovered was that the major reason for success in life was a particular attitude of mind. This attitude was based around their longer-term goal setting and activities. Banfield dubbed this *"long time perspective"*. Dr Banfield discovered that those individuals who have a longer-term view of what they want and how they want to achieve it (in every minute detail) and start straight away to work *inch by inch* every day without fail towards that goal, end up being the most successful individuals in whatever field of endeavour they embark upon regardless of their background. Rainmakers know that the long time perspective incorporates two distinct, yet related concepts—vision and goals.

People use the terms vision and goals interchangeably, however, the two are very different in meaning and function. The two terms are also interdependent. Real and lasting success is only possible if the two work in tandem.

Are Rainmakers visionaries or goal-setters? Well, the answer to that question is they *have to be both*! Most people have a natural disposition towards either being a visionary or a goal-setter and not necessarily both. A goal-setter is process and task oriented, focusing on achieving an aim within a certain timeframe and determining the steps towards that aim: the goal. On the other hand, a visionary has a clear picture in mind of how things should be. It's a picture of an on-going state of being that has no time span and is not usually accompanied with a set of pragmatic steps of how to get there.

Rainmakers know that they have to be good at displaying both. Therefore, they are acutely aware of what they are good at and work hard on their aptitude for the weaker concept.

What do you want to achieve in the next 5 to 10 years? What are you willing to do (or to even give up) NOW to enable that to happen? What type of clients do you want to service? What type of relationships do you want to have with these clients? What are you willing to do (or to even give up) NOW to enable that to happen? How much wealth do you really want to create? What are you willing to do (or to even give up) NOW to enable that to happen?

Remember:
Always begin with the end in mind!

Insight 12

The Habit of a Lifetime

Developing and maintaining the right habits is critical to success at work and in life. Personal growth guru, Dr Stephen Covey in his famous 1989 book *The Seven Habits of Highly Effective People*, stressed the need for acquiring life-changing habits such as always being proactive, thinking win-win and beginning with the end in mind. Having these habits is certainly fundamental to one accomplishing their goals; however, a quotation by Benjamin Franklin comes to mind: "Your net worth to the world is usually determined by what remains after your bad habits are subtracted from your good ones".

You must be aware of your negative thought patterns and their pathway to you developing bad habits that limit the actualisation of your goals and debilitate your life. The creation of good habits without the destruction of bad ones only creates a lack of harmony in your quest for success.

Think of habits such as procrastination, lack of attention to detail, counting your chickens before they hatch, being impatient, not qualifying thoroughly, gossiping, being unprepared, making sweeping assumptions, lacking self-confidence, fear, under-delegating, over-delegating, indecision, unnecessary work overload, not thinking creatively or laterally, lack of trust in others etc. These habits and many others can destroy relationships, limit careers and keep you from attaining the kind of financial freedom you deserve.

Search your life, regularly write down *all* your current habits and when examining them ask yourself one question: *"Does this habit serve me?"* If your answer is no, develop the 21-day habit of breaking that habit.

> Remember: The blueprint of your life is your character, and this in turn is the sum total of your habits. Make them serve you.

Insight 13

The Folly of Lamentations

Kampfschwimmer. That's the name of the infamous German naval commandos. They are amongst the top special operations forces on the planet. The motto of this elite squad is taken from one of the old Prussian virtues: *Lerne leiden ohne zu klagen*, which in English means, "Learn to Suffer without Complaining".

It seems that complaining, moaning, griping, grumbling, whining, lamenting is a favourite pastime of many a salesperson. When I ask salespeople, "Why are you constantly moaning?" the answer always appears to be something along the lines of "...it's political, you won't understand..." or "...I need to vent or I'll go crazy".

The Rainmaker's definition of a complaint is *the creation of stifling negativity that leads nowhere.*

Nothing positive or progressive occurs when we complain, even to ourselves. Neuroscience shows us that it leads to a gloomy mind and a stressful body. The two last things the Rainmaker needs when pursuing success through excellence. There is an old saying, "If you don't have something positive to say then don't say anything". In the same vein, if you can't think positively then try not to think!

Life in today's hyper-competitive world can be tough. If one doesn't take care, one's thoughts and words can make one lose sight of the prize ahead and become derailed. Rainmakers guard their minds like fortresses. They literally cannot afford to feel bad about anything—the little things as well as the big ones. They are completely aggressive in shutting down little weeds of negativity and find real solutions to the big challenges that will *always* appear along the way to success. Rainmakers stay clear of habitual complainers, as negativity can be one of the most infectious diseases in the world. It's so much easier to become negative because a colleague displays negativity than to be inspired by someone positive.

The trick Rainmakers use to become and stay positive is very simple. *They cultivate gratitude.* I know it sounds a bit esoteric, but it works. The more you are grateful for everything—your health, your life, your family, other people—the more you will find it difficult to complain. It's like gratitude and moaning are diametrically opposed. The Rainmaker's definition of gratitude is the inverse of the definition of the complaint, *the creation of empowering positivity that can only lead to success.* Don't just try and stop complaining about things—practice and master the subtle art of gratitude in everything.

> # Remember: Ask yourself- What do I need to be grateful for today?

Insight 14

Risky Business

The author of the famous book *The Road Less Travelled*, M. Scott Peck, once said: "We must be willing to fail and to appreciate the truth that often life is not a problem to be solved, but a mystery to be lived".

The poignant phrase that stands out for me in that quotation is *"willing to fail"*. M. Scott Peck could have used a number of adjectives to qualify failure such as "prepare to fail" or "don't be afraid to fail". But to be willing to fail seems to have so much more punch to it. It's like one is actually taunting failure, saying *"I'm willing to bring it on if you are"*.

The fear of failure is the single biggest target-killing commission-buster in our game and though the title of Susan Jeffers' book is "Feel the Fear and Do it Anyway", It's hard, when simply trying not to be afraid, to really push the boundaries of what you are capable of as a sales professional. But to be *willing* to fail—now that has something extra, it has the impetus to empower you to grab failure by the neck and wring success out of it.

Thomas Watson, who I mentioned in the *Rock Solid* insight, was not afraid of failure. Watson once said, "If you want to double your rate of success, double your rate of failure". Watson literally lived by his words. In 1892 at the age of 18, Watson travelled from farm to farm peddling pianos, organs and sewing machines. He earned $10 a week, only to find out that his boss had duped him as he could have been earning $70 a week if he had been working on commission instead of salary. Watson then quit and moved to Buffalo and took a job selling sewing machines for Wheeler & Wilcox with little success so he began selling shares of the Buffalo Building and Loan Company, however his partner, C.B. Barron, disappeared with the firm's money and Watson's commissions. Watson then decided to open a butcher shop in Buffalo but before long that failed too. So he joined National Cash Register (NCR) and, to be fair, Watson had a lot of success at NCR ultimately rising to become the second in command of NCR after NCR's President, John H. Patterson, but ultimately Watson was fired from that job. It was only in 1914 at IBM that Watson, now 40, used all of the experience from his five previous failures to make a massive and lasting success of his life and the lives of many others. Thomas Watson had no problem with failing to succeed.

Anything worth achieving involves risk, particularly the risk of failure. Risk is the single common denominator for capitalism and enterprise. Without risk, financial freedom and everything wonderful that comes with it will always be a wish away. However, if you embrace risk and are willing to do whatever it takes to achieve (including fail), to be better, to smash targets, to create wealth, then it will all surely come to pass.

> Remember: Your willingness to fail equates to your acceptance to succeed.

Insight 15

If You Shoot, You Just Might Score

How does a pilot or a shipmaster know where he is going and how he intends to get there if he hasn't plotted a course *in advance* of the journey?

One takes an unnecessary risk jumping into a situation without thinking and planning the outcome and the process. Taking on a sales target is no different.

It is one thing to have (be given) a target and quite another to have a firm goal set in your mind, in your psyche, to achieve that target as well as formulating a cast-iron strategy, both of which will increase your probability of reaching that goal.

Here are some things to think about:

- **Dream big:** Diana Scharf Hunt once wrote: "Goals are dreams with deadlines". Your goals have to start with dreams, so dream BIG. Let your imagination run wild: money, cars, holidays, charity, family, hobby. Whatever you want…dream it.

- **Write your goals down:** A goal in your head stays a dream. Writing them down *crystallises* the thought. Something happens when you write things down in black and white— it's like signals move to your subconscious commanding it to begin marching towards your goals.

- **Read your goals:** Preferably aloud. Read them with emotion and feeling, as if they really mean something to you.

- **Visualise your goals:** When you form a mental picture of what you want to achieve and how overachieving on your target can get you there, make it clear and vivid in your mind's eye. If it's a holiday, see the beach, smell the sea salt in the air, hear the waves crashing on the shoreline. Do this constantly every day.

- **Believe you will achieve:** Don't just develop goals for the sake of it. Believe they will become a reality within the timescale you set. Make your belief a conviction so that when things look bleak, your anchor is your firm belief that you WILL hit targets and achieve your goals.

- **Rewrite your goals daily:** Why would you simply write them at the beginning of the sales year and forget them? Remember, writing them down is magical, so rewrite them every day.

- **Formulate a strategy to achieve targets:** An example could be the "numbers game" strategy I'll outline in "*The Benefit of Mathematics*", or it could be doing a SWOT analysis of your professional self and making decisions from there.

- **Show flexibility:** Constantly review and adjust your strategy throughout the year. You don't want to find that at the end of the year you realise you should have done things a little differently. Be flexible and honest with yourself.

If you set goals, then truly believe and trust in them, formulate a strategy to achieve them, and be flexible in your approach. You will surely over-achieve.

> # Remember: The goal posts are wider than you think!

Insight 16

In Your Prime

A prime number is a natural number that is only divisible by 1 and itself. Apart from prime numbers, 1 and 0, any other number is a composite number. Therefore, if you begin to divide a composite number, you ultimately arrive at a prime number, 1, or 0.

We know that without goals, one will have no motivation or direction in life. But there are goals and there are *goals*. I like to split goals into *prime goals* and *composite goals*. The prime goal is the foundational, fundamental goal in which all other goals in that arena naturally fall into place. Say, for example, you had two goals: to put your children through private school and to be a successful Rainmaker within a year. Which is the prime goal and which is the composite goal? Which goal naturally creates which? To be a successful Rainmaker within a year will only serve to provide you with more than enough wealth to put your children through private school. The prime goal requires focus, dedication, willpower and massive action, whilst the composite goal just requires a decision, as the means to deliver a composite goal is derived from the prime goal.

When examining your goals, it's important to thoroughly understand them so as to decide where to centre your attention. The great Rainmaker Zig Ziglar once said, "What you get by achieving your goals is just as important as what you *become* by achieving your goals". This quotation demonstrates where to pour in your passion: *self-actualisation*—the realisation of your potential. If there ever were a prime of prime goals, this would be it. Everything else happens once you *become*. All your prime goals should be pointing towards making you a better professional, spouse, parent, friend or business partner—in fact, a better human being. All other goals will naturally flow from there. Depleting your precious mental, physical and subconscious energies in chasing composite goals alone will only prolong the road less travelled to success.

> # Remember: Concentrate on the prime goals whilst in your prime and your future will stay bright.

Insight 17

The Aggression in Progress

You have goals. You have targets. You have plans and a strategy to achieve them. You have the resources and the time to do it—and to do it well. You have the desire, the burning desire to do what it takes to become the Rainmaker. You know you have to create value, not just communicate it, so as to sustain long-term profitable relationships with customers. In short, you know what it takes.

The question then arises, what is the right attitude to have that will empower you to achieve all of these things and more? The answer is this: You need to be *aggressively progressive*.

Aggression as a noun does have negativity about it. But as an adjective, or in this case, an adverb, it can be defined as *assertive, bold and energetic*. Your attitude to your work, your career, your targets and the sales process, needs to be *aggressively progressive*. Rainmakers kick distractive habits with aggression; they focus on acquiring the right skills to be successful with aggression; they face their aggressive targets and surpass them through aggression.

Make no mistake about this, I do not in any way mean aggression in the physical sense of the word, but certainly you need to be extremely aggressive in the *mental* sense. This is how you turn your burning desire to achieve into massive action. Indeed, this is how you create that burning desire in the first place.

The force needed for a plane lift off and get to cruising altitude in the sky is immense. The four Rolls Royce engines need to aggressively progress the vessel off the ground. It is no different with Rainmakers.

Use an aggressively progressive mind-set to push yourself forward to overachievement. Take no prisoners when striving to be the best you can. Earl Henry Blaik, the famous American football coach, once said: "Good guys are a dime a dozen, but an aggressive leader is priceless". It's time to bring out the leader in you and make it happen!

> # Remember:
> # Your attitude
> # determines
> # your altitude!

Insight 18

Your Cards

In poker-playing circles, there is an old saying: "It's not the hand you are dealt that counts, it's how you play it". In these difficult economic times, it is tempting to play the blame game: it's the economy, our products are not good enough, our competitors are cheaper, my targets are too high, marketing are not listening to me, we never seem to have any training, this or that department doesn't co-operate…the list can go on and on.

Around two thousand years ago, the Greek Stoic philosopher Epictetus shared the same sentiment as the poker players by saying: "It's not what happens to you, but how you react to it that matters". Some of the most successful business people, professionals and Rainmakers didn't have the best advantages in life: they certainly suffered many difficult setbacks, and conditions surrounding them were indeed far from ideal. What sets them apart however is that they all looked *within* and focused on what they *did* have to bring about the change needed to make things happen for themselves.

Your mind is the most powerful gift you have and the best thing about it is that it's all yours. Be warned though, fill it with negativity and distractions and you will go nowhere fast. Be aware of your mind, develop it and guard it from incapacitating thoughts. If you *think* it, you can *achieve* it. To believe is your choice.

Remember:
Winners not
only see the
glass half-
full,
they fill it up!

Insight 19

The Self-Con-Artist

Self-confidence is an interesting phenomenon. On the one hand you know it when you see it, on the other hand you can't accurately quantify a description when you witness it. One might say "that guy oozes confidence" while another might say "there is something about the way she came across" or any number of other observations.

One thing we do know however is that self-confidence is paramount to our jobs, our businesses and our lives. Prospects buy your services *because* they buy into you. They put their trust in you. Your customer will never be confident in you if you are not confident in yourself, your firm, your products and services and *them—the customer.*

Lots of business and personal development gurus have come up with a myriad of ways to improve your self-confidence but I have three favourites that I think are worth sharing with you:

- **Like yourself**: If you don't like who you are, what you are and who you are becoming, it's difficult to *pretend* you are confident. How do you like yourself? Simple...by saying to yourself, with feeling, that you like yourself at least 50 times a day. Sounds mad I know, but try it.

- **Know your stuff:** It's difficult for the mind to be at ease when selling to prospects and you not knowing *what* you are selling and *how* you are selling it, and *why* they might buy it. To be a professional, you have to always be a student of your profession.

- **Visualise. Visualise. Visualise:** The mind influences everything you do and say. If you "trick" the mind into believing that you ooze confidence, guess what? Somehow, you'll ooze confidence. Before a meeting, presentation or phone call, close your eyes and visualise in vivid colour how you will come across and the positive outcome of the event. The deeper and more intense you visualise, the more likely the mind will blur imagination and reality in theatre.

> Remember: Confidence, like wealth, is a shared pool. Tap into it and we'll all be winners.

Insight 20

Continuous Fashion

Kaizen (改善). Japanese for continuous improvement. Direct translation is *"change for the better"*. In the late 80s to early 90s the management consulting craze was *quality through continuous improvement*. The guru who championed quality was a guy called Dr. W. Edwards Demming who worked with post-war Japanese corporations to increase their productivities to levels unheard of at that time.

At the heart of this philosophy is Kaizen. Yet the concept of continuous improvement is not new. Thousands of years earlier, Socrates once said: "Employ your time in improving yourself by other men's writings so that you shall come easily by what others have laboured hard for".

Your career never stands still. It careers onwards. You know, the word career comes from the Latin word *carrera* which means **race** (now you know where Porsche got the 911 name from)? Your career is a race, a pursuit for excellence, for satisfaction, for wealth and well-being. In order to achieve all this, you must improve all the time. You must never stop stepping up your game.

Remember:
Adopt personal
Kaizen in your life
and career
and you will
be rewarded
handsomely.

Insight 21

Believe! Not Make-Believe.

It's impossible to achieve anything worthwhile without self-belief, without the ability to say to yourself "I will achieve this, I am *going* to make this happen!" and have an unflinching faith in those words. Let me give you an analogy.

Two friends, one is at work and one is at home. The one at home starts watching the football match live on a sports channel. It's an intense game, and by half time the team that both friends support is 1:4 down with little hope of a real comeback. However, in the second half, the losing team come back strong, and slowly but surely start making a recovery and miraculously score the last two goals in the final three minutes of the game, with the final score being 5:4 to the team both friends supported, heart-stopping stuff!

The friend comes back from work eager not to know what happened and they both sit down to watch the recording of the game. Imagine the difference in attitudes, since the first friend knows what to expect and is calm through the heart-wrenching first half and the anxious second half.

The relaxed attitude of this friend is the attitude that Rainmakers display within themselves day in and day out *whatever the circumstance.* They are cool, calm and collected with an unshakable belief in themselves. Do you believe in yourself, your products and your company? Do you believe that you can achieve your sales targets and personal goals even when all evidence appears to the contrary? Do you believe?

Remember:

Belief

precedes

Success.

Insight 22

Sitting Uncomfortably isn't a Bad Thing

The world is a big place. I don't mean the physical world, though the globe seems to be shrinking by the day. I mean the world of experiences. This world is huge, infinitely huge. Yet the world of *our* experiences is infinitesimally small in comparison. However, the path to personal and professional growth exists within this expansive world of new and limitless experiences and not in the small and limited paradigm we create for ourselves. This world exists outside of our comfort zone.

Rainmakers may sometimes appear superhuman with their impressive display of a myriad of skills and their apparent fearlessness, but every Rainmaker will tell you that deep down, they are just as ordinary, fragile and vulnerable as everyone else. The difference is that Rainmakers know that skills and attitudes are carved out of experiences, and therefore immersing themselves in bigger, bolder and more challenging experiences will serve to develop them in many ways. There is a catch though. The gatekeeper.

Try and imagine the two worlds of experiences I stated earlier. The small world of your experiences is a small room with a big comfy sofa in the middle and a single door. On the other side of that door lies the big world of new and powerful experiences and the path to success. But at the door stands the dreaded gatekeeper called FUD (fear, uncertainty, doubt). Now, FUD is a real smooth talker and every time you try to venture through that door FUD finds a way to talk you out of it. FUD uses every tactic at its disposal to convince you to sit back in that comfortable chair in the middle of your small room. Rainmakers meet exactly the same situation every time they challenge themselves to a new experience, but Rainmakers also *know* exactly what's on the other side of that door. They also believe that each new experience ends up in making their small room expand in itself. Therefore, with this knowledge, they must ignore FUD every time, as FUD only represents our fight-or-flight lizard brain and not our desire to be the best we can possibly be. The sequence of your journey should be:

comfortable – uncomfortable – comfortable – repeat. This is the only way to develop into the Rainmaker you will become.

Remember:

Life begins at the end of your comfort zone.

Insight 23

Nerve Endings

You are about to make that all-important phone call, attend that pivotal meeting or make that critical presentation and yet you have that horrible feeling in your stomach. You almost feel sick, your mind is suddenly void of all knowledge and memory and you're constantly thinking about how badly you are likely to perform… which only makes you feel worse…

Rainmakers constantly find themselves in situations where their nerves can get the better of them. No matter how much experience one has, nerves can appear at any time and if entertained and not dealt with, can affect the sales event and possibly the outcome. Confucius once said: "If you look into your own heart, and you find nothing wrong there, what is there to worry about? What is there to fear?"

It is important to remember that having nerves is simply a biochemical reaction in your body brought about by your subconscious. Adrenaline is pumped into your bloodstream and this is what gives you that queasy feeling in your stomach. Your heart rate also increases and your blood vessels constrict. This is not a good place to be if ignored or worse still if you panic, as you will only increase that cycle.

The adrenaline is actually there to make you more *focussed*. It's there to sharpen your mind, preparing your nervous system to react quickly. As primitives, adrenaline existed to enable our fight-

or-flight response, as Rainmakers, it exists to enable us to think on our feet and recall everything we know and have trained for. You should therefore *welcome* the adrenaline rush and use it the way it was designed to be used. One way to quickly calm down and yet benefit from all the positives of adrenaline is to *breathe*. Yes, it's that simple. Breathe. Breathing properly will fill your bloodstream with oxygenated blood, which will rush to your brain and will instantly calm you down, whilst you still stay sharp for your big moment. Follow this routine:

- Take a four-second, slow and deep breath in through your nose, pushing your diaphragm down as much as possible.

- Hold your breath down using your diaphragm muscles for two seconds.

- Slowly breathe out through your mouth for four seconds.

- Repeat the process once more.

That's it. You will see that straight away you become much calmer and at the same time ready to do what you need to do and the best thing about this routine is that you can perform it anywhere.

> Remember: There is power in your nerves. It's yours to harness.

Insight 24

Thales' Answer

"You take the blue pill: the story ends, you wake up in your bed and believe whatever you want to believe. You take the red pill: you stay in Wonderland and I show you how deep the rabbit-hole goes".

In the Wachowski brothers' 1999 film *The Matrix*, Laurence Fishburne's character, Morpheus, presents Neo, Keanu Reeves' character, with a choice. That choice leads Neo to many things throughout the Matrix trilogy but the number one gift *"the choice of the pills"* gave Neo was *self-awareness.*

Self-awareness is indeed a gift. Understand and develop it and you will go on to achieve your prime goal: self-actualisation. Abraham Maslow, in his 1954 book *Motivation and Personality* wrote, "Whereas the average individuals often have not the slightest idea of what they are, of what they want, of what their own opinions are, self-actualizing individuals have superior awareness of their own impulses, desires, opinions, and subjective reactions in general".

Don't however confuse self-awareness with self-consciousness. Self-consciousness makes you see through the lens of how *you* perceive others perceiving you. Being entangled in the messy web of that double lens will only weaken you and will undoubtedly lower your self-esteem. The lower your self-esteem, the further away your goals will always seem to be.

Self-awareness, on the other hand, is an acute understanding of you, by you and for you. If you realise who you really are in the cold light of day—your strengths, weaknesses, deepest fears, aspirations, historical baggage, attitude, impulses, shame and guilt, you have a basis to develop yourself, to grow, all the time knowing how far you are coming. Self-awareness thus empowers you to be better, to achieve. If you don't read and understand the instruction manual, how will you get the machine to do what you want it to do? You *are* the machine. The instruction manual is written and used through your self-awareness.

Rainmakers are acutely aware of who they are and what they are capable of. They know that if they don't harness this gift, they will be like tumbleweeds blowing in the wind—destination: nowhere and anywhere! Take the time out to reflect on who you are versus who you want to be. Seek the red pill, and see just how far you can go. The choice is yours.

> # Remember: Be a high definition colour version of yourself and not everyone else's perceived black and white version of you.

Insight 25

Hold the Fort

One of my favourite movies is Ridley Scott's *Gladiator*. I love the classic revenge plot mixed with pain, passion and a dash of patriotism. One solemn scene struck me. The stage is set for Commodus, the son of Caesar to murder his father. He tells his father, "You wrote to me once, listing the four chief virtues: wisdom, justice, fortitude and temperance. As I read the list, I knew I had none of them..."

Those virtues immediately demonstrated to me all the character traits one needs to become a leader, a teacher, a warrior...a Rainmaker.

Rainmakers need to develop and exercise all four virtues to be successful. If, however, you possessed none and had to start on one, it would be *fortitude*. Around 380 BC, Plato taught these virtues to his pupils. All four are documented in his Socratic dialogue, *The Republic*. Plato focused on fortitude for his warrior class—the future leaders of armies, heads of military conquests.

What is fortitude and why is it so important to the Rainmaker?

The *Oxford English Dictionary* defines fortitude as simply: *"courage in pain or adversity"*. I simply see it as strength of mind in all situations. Make no mistake about it, being a Rainmaker can be hard. It's a difficult, lonely, uphill road to success with a lot of bumps, twists and turns along the way and countless setbacks. It really is not for the faint-hearted. The majority of salespeople new to the profession leave it after a short time because they simply cannot hack it. There is a constant pressure from all sides. Even if you are successful, it's momentary; as the old sales adage says: *"you are only as good as your last sale"*.

If, however, you focus on the skills needed to succeed such as adding value to the customers, building the pipeline and always acting with integrity, all the benefits of this noble profession will be yours. To do that, you must possess strength of mind. You must develop it, practise it; you must protect it.

Fortitude will see you through the times when management are saying you are not good enough. Fortitude will see you through when it looks like nothing is about to drop. Fortitude will see you through when personal problems threaten to get in the way of your quest for success. Fortitude will see you through when you can't seem to get any support from anywhere. Fortitude will see you through when the dark days look like they are never-ending. Fortitude will always see you through.

Remember:
Hold your mind firm and you will witness the best life has to offer.

Insight 26

Ahead of the Learning Curve

We currently live in an amazing time in history. We can get to anywhere on the planet in a matter of hours; we can communicate with anyone and everyone, anywhere in the world in an instant; we can truly discern and be responsible for our actions. One thing however that makes this point in history worthwhile is our access to knowledge and information. It's everywhere and at our fingertips.

So how can we tap into this vast reservoir of knowledge and use it to become what we desire, which is to be that Rainmaker who uses the skills developed to make him or her better, to make business better, to make the world better?

There is an academic or professional course for everything, absolutely everything. If you look hard enough, there is a book or e-book written that can teach you whatever it is you want and need to learn. The availability of knowledge is only as abundant or as limited as you perceive it to be.

One of the world's leading motivational speakers, Tony Robbins, was actually a teenager and homeless when he had a chance encounter with another motivational speaker called Jim Rohn. From that moment on, Tony decided he wanted to become a world-class motivational speaker. He had no formal education beyond high school, but he did do something well—he took learning seriously. Tony went on any course he could, read every book he could in his chosen field (literally several hundred books and publications) and he took this knowledge and absorbed it. Within a year he was a millionaire. Today, Tony is one of the greatest speakers of his generation and he even owns an island in Fiji.

The point of the story is that if you want to grow in a particular area in order to be better and more effective, then be proactive and seek out how to do it. Pay for a course, buy *and read* that book, register for that online seminar. Whatever you learn, you will always take it with you so it's certainly worth investing in acquiring the knowledge you need to be better.

> Remember:
> Your most important
> investment is in
> yourself..

Insight 27

What's Your One Move?

There's a saying I once heard that has forever stuck in my head. It goes: *"life is full of obstacle illusions"*. When I initially came across this saying, I thought it was a good play on words. On deeper reflection, I find it's not just a cool saying but a profound and true one. Challenges and setbacks always litter the path to achievement and success. I suppose that is why it is called "the road less travelled". The biggest, baddest, ugliest and most stubborn obstacles, however, are your own *perceived* weaknesses and handicaps. They have the power to stop you dead in your tracks—*if you give them permission to*. The good news? They are just mirages, illusions, smoke and mirrors, tricks of the mind. Many a time, your biggest weakness can become your biggest strength.

Take, for example, the old fable of a ten-year-old boy who decided to take up judo despite the fact that he had lost his left arm in a serious car accident. The boy started lessons with an old Japanese judo master. The boy began making progress, but could not understand why after three whole months of training the master had taught him only one move. "Sensei," the boy finally asked, "Shouldn't I be learning more moves?"

"This is the only move you know, but this is the only move you'll ever need to know," the sensei quietly replied. Not quite understanding, but believing in his teacher, the boy kept training. Several months later, the sensei took the boy to his first tournament.

Surprising himself, the boy easily won his first two matches. The third match proved to be more difficult, but after some time, his opponent became impatient and charged; the boy deftly used his one move to win the match. Still amazed by his success, the boy was now in the finals. This time, his opponent was bigger, stronger, and more experienced. For a while, the boy appeared to be outclassed by his opponent. Concerned that the boy might get hurt, the referee called a time-out. He was about to stop the match when the sensei intervened. "No," the sensei insisted, "Let him continue". Soon after the match resumed, his opponent made a critical mistake: he dropped his guard. Instantly, the boy used his move to pin him. The boy won the match and the tournament. He was the champion.

On the way home, the boy and sensei reviewed every move in every match. The boy then summoned the courage to ask what was really on his mind. "Sensei, how did I win the tournament with only one move?"

"You won for two reasons," the sensei answered. "First, you've mastered one of the most difficult throws in all of judo. And second, the only known defence for that move is for your opponent to grab your left arm".

Rainmakers are in the business of self-improvement, and some of the biggest leaps towards your goals can be achieved by tackling head on your biggest weaknesses, personal or professional. You have three choices available to you. Firstly, you can believe the illusion and stay where you are, wishing and hoping for the forever-elusive progress to come your way. Secondly, you can overcome your weakness by changing your perception of it, your thoughts and behavioural patterns. Thirdly, if the weakness is a real handicap, as with the ten-year-old boy, find ways to turn it into a strength.

Be honest with yourself: jot down your weaknesses, be they mental or physical, find ways to change them or develop new skills to counterbalance them. Either way, ignore the illusions of obstacles and grab hold of the reality of progress.

Remember: Stop staring at the non-existent palm trees in the middle of the desert and start making it rain.

Insight 28

The United States of You

Think of a time when you seemed to do everything right. Maybe it was the way you handled a particular meeting or a prospecting call. Every word, action and thought just all seemed to gel in harmony. You couldn't go wrong. You were in flow, in the zone. World famous motivational expert Anthony Robbins calls this phenomenon *peak state*.

State is an interesting concept. On one hand it's everywhere, constant, yet transparent, as you are always in state—positive, inconsequential or negative. On the other hand, understanding and using state is so crucial to the success of our business, our careers, our lives, our destinies. But what exactly is state? Well, the *Oxford English Dictionary* defines state as: *the particular condition that someone or something is in at a specific time.* So, for example, one could say, "look at the state of you" or "He was in a right state". The powerful thing about state is that it directly affects *outcomes*. It is the outcomes that Rainmakers are really interested in.

So here's the big question: If state influences results then how can we manage our state when it really matters? *How can we get ourselves to be at our superlative state at will?*

We all know the famous "show me the money" scene in Cameron Crowe's 1996 film *Jerry Maguire,* where Cuba Gooding, Jr's character Rod Tidwell tests Tom Cruise's character, Jerry's resolve over the phone. Rod pushes Jerry to be more and more vocal on the phone ending with Jerry screaming "show me the money!" and other interesting phrases. When thinking about that scene and what Rod Tidwell was trying to do, it occurred to me that he was trying to get Jerry to *alter his state*. Initially, Jerry was not overly enthused to Rod Tidwell agreeing to keep Jerry as his agent. Rod realised that in order to change Jerry's state of mind, he *first* had to change his physical state by getting him to scream at the top of his voice. Once the state changes, the outcome changes.

Rainmakers understand that the right state is the foundation of performance. Therefore, they must become masters of their own state. Rainmakers realise that like actors on the stage, it is not enough to know your stuff, but one has to be in the right state, the right zone, when it truly matters—at that meeting, throughout that presentation, during that call, in that seminar. They use motion and emotion to get into state, they recall past peak states in their minds and recreate them again and again in reality. They study *Neuro-Linguistic Programming* techniques to master achieving state at will. Do what Rainmakers do. Learn the art of getting in state.

> Remember: The cumulative state of your business is a mirror image of the consistent management of your state.

Insight 29

Tomorrow Tomorrow Tomorrow

There is an old saying that *procrastination is the thief of time*. It's the one thing, which, if left unchecked, can do the most damage to your sales, targets and career. Yet it is one of the hardest things to shake off. It's like a virus: it starts off unnoticed and then slowly multiplies, making it increasingly difficult to extinguish. Putting things off then becomes a habit that really starts to take hold of your work life and can strangle it completely.

The point is that when you finally get around to doing things, it normally is because you *have to* and you are now running against the clock and that can only mean that the quality of your *output* can be compromised. The only thing of equity we possess as Rainmakers is our output: *the results of what we do* such as phone calls we make, the meetings we prepare, the proposals and presentations we create. If these are less than excellent as components, the total sum product of our efforts begin to fall into jeopardy.

Here are a number of ideas to consider about how to deal with procrastination:

- **Be aware:** Be acutely aware. This gremlin is never far from you. You need to be honest with yourself and know that it can affect even the smallest of decisions.

- **Write down your yearly goals daily:** Repeating the process of evaluating your goals on a daily basis will fortify your mind with the things you have to do to achieve them.

- **Make a "to do list":** This may sound obvious but we normally do one in our heads, which can only make it easy for procrastination to decimate this mental register. Stating things in black and white will go a long way in helping you getting things done.

- **Important doesn't necessarily mean urgent:** Yes, you need to fire-fight sometimes—however, the more you do the *important* stuff earlier, the less you will fire-fight later. Identify what's important but not necessarily urgent, such as cold calling or preparing early for a presentation, and work on those tasks first.

- **Reward yourself:** Pat yourself on the back for working hard and getting the important stuff out of the way. This positive gesture will only reinforce your positive motivational state for the next time.

Dealing with procrastination is a lifelong endeavour but we can *form the habit of kicking the habit* of procrastination if we stay focused.

> # Remember: Destroy the thief of time and time will reward you.

Insight 30

Where Do You Sign?

Have you ever seen the bright new actor or the promising musician, the budding entrepreneur or the ambitious professional and you somehow *know* this person will do well? This person will go far. But for the life of you, you can't think exactly why. You cannot put your finger on it, but there is something special about that individual. You recognise that "specialness" every time you see that actor on TV, hear that musician on the radio or interact with that professional in some way. They have a *signature*.

Like your personality, fingerprint or iris, your signature is unique to you and you alone. Every time you sign a cheque or a letter, you display a representation of you. Only you!

Question: What representation of you are *you* displaying to the commercial world? Is this representation consistent? What signature do you leave with your prospects and clients?

People buy people. It seems an obvious statement. A mantra often used in sales. One would be mistaken, however, to think that this means people buy just a personality. If that is indeed the case, if you are a "people" person then everyone will flock to buy from you. Not so. People, committees, companies, organisations buy the signature. This is the all-encompassing uniqueness that only you can provide. It is the culmination of many hours of learning, relearning, practising and refining your profession. Your Rainmaker's signature also comprises knowledge, passion, commitment, hard work, vision, friendship, service and humility, yet a pride in what you do. The embodiment of all these factors surrounded by a strong spirit of excellence will create a representation unique to you that customers will buy into again and again.

Remember:
Rainmakers
never leave home
without their
signature. What's
Yours?

Insight 31

Doing the Nearly Impossible Everyday

Here is a simple equation: *Lack of growth = Death*. This is true on many levels. If one stops meeting challenges and developing when one retires, it's an early grave. If businesses remain stagnant in today's environment, the receivers beckon. If the salesperson doesn't consistently grow in skills, in their pipeline, in orders, in relationships, in the size of their network; then it's goodbye to their job, possibly their career and their dreams. These are the harsh realities of life, which can be viewed as a good thing since it spurs us on to grow. *To stretch.*

On Monday, August 15th, 2016 at the Olympic Stadium in Engenho de Dentro, Brazil's Thiago Braz da Silva, appeared from nowhere to claim the gold medal and set a new Olympic pole vault record. Da Silva failed his first attempt at 5.75m. On his second attempt, he cleared 5.93m which was his personal best. Defending Olympic pole vault champion, France's Renaud Lavillenie had raised the bar by clearing 5.98m. Da Silva knew he had one chance for gold for Brazil, in Brazil and go down in history for Brazilian track and field fans, so he *decided to stretch* with all his being and might and clear the bar at 6.03m, a full 10cm above his personal best to set a new Olympic record. That is the power of stretching!

Stretching is the key to growth. It's the fuel that drives the engine of success. I like to define stretching as *doing the nearly impossible every day.* Think of something in your everyday job you think is impossible to do or at least really difficult to achieve, such as positively aggressively getting that meeting from that difficult client, closing that huge deal, pushing clients for referrals, insisting to yourself that you *will* double your pipeline within a month by hook or by crook (OK, less of the crook), deciding that you will drastically increase your close rate. Now imagine one puts a gun to your head and says, "…if you don't hit your yearly target within six months of the start of the year I will pull the trigger". Are you going to say, "OK, I'll try?" Of course not! You are going to say, "Yes I will…I must!" When the mind is focussed, the impossible is achieved for the simple reason that it's the mind itself that defines what impossible is in the first place, it's called your *paradigm.*

Stretching is the single characteristic all successful people have in common, worldwide and in all cultures. Pushing your mind, body and soul to their very limits to attain a goal is your passport to high achievement. The weird thing is that it's actually easy. The hard part, the really hard part, is *deciding* to seriously go for it in the first place. You have to undergo a mind shift to start with. The battleground is in the mind.

If the mind comes up with an objection to you stretching yourself—say, for example, you feel you want get out there and cold call prospects consistently but the mind says *"you can't"*, a simple reply to yourself is: "But if I could, how would I go about it?" Use this statement anytime you have any doubts: *"But if I could…"* Because you *can,* you just have to condition yourself to accept that very fact.

Stretch yourself, push yourself, dive into the challenges, let nothing and no one (especially yourself) stop you from making it. Explore the outer limits of what *you* think is possible. Do this today and every day. Don't ever let the mind fool you into relaxing by thinking you're doing fine. *Never* stop stretching…*ever.* Rainmakers never do.

> Remember: How far you pull the catapult back is a lot less than how far the stone goes on release.

Insight 32

Team You

Imagine your sales manager was Grant Cardone, who had all the time in the world to show you how to overachieve on the numbers. Imagine how successful you would be if you turned to Anthony Robbins for advice on personal development and peak performance. Imagine how many more deals you would close if you had a weekly session with master negotiator Henry Kissinger or how much more passionate and involving your presentations would be after spending time with Steve Jobs.

Watching my two boys grow up is a real privilege and joy. One thing that particularly strikes me is the way they are like sponges and all they really want to do is latch on to someone that inspires them to learn and be better. Should we as adults, be any different?

Author Auliq Ice once said, "Life is constantly teaching us that we are mirrors of one another and that no one is an island". Whatever stage we are at in our professional and personal life, receiving advice, encouragement, edification and inspiration from those who are ahead of us provides the growth spurts we need to be successful.

I have not heard of a Rainmaker, entrepreneur, Olympic gold medallist, Nobel Prize winner or indeed anyone who has achieved lasting success, who does not have one or more mentors in their lives—it is one of success' critical ingredients.

However, obtaining a mentor only tells a third of the story.

Another third is the inverse: being a mentor. Teaching, sharing and inspiring others coming after you only serves to enrich your own journey exponentially. The final third is the influence of your peers. These are carefully chosen and like-minded individuals that share common goals and attitudes towards advancement.

I refer to all three components as *Team You*, and if you design this team thoughtfully and cultivate it properly, it will propel you to the top of your game at an astonishing rate.

Team You will not come to you. You have to go out and seek your team. Be bold and look for the right mentors for you, take on the right protégé and work on your relationships with your peers (friends, work colleagues, industry partners and even competitors) and hold on to those who are like-minded, positive, trustworthy and most importantly, able to challenge you on a deep and meaningful level.

> # Remember:
> ## An individual can achieve good things but great things can only be achieved for the individual by a team of individuals.

Insight 33

Your Very Own Personal Power

Question: If you had all the information about what to do and how to do it, you knew exactly how to transform yourself into the superstar sales professional you want to be, and how to earn the big commissions you deserve; what would you do next?

Where is the power to turn what's in your head into reality? How do you get from knowing it to actually living it? The answer is in the little phrase "to decide".

Decision comes from the Latin word *caedere* which literally means to "cut off". Think about these words: suicide, homicide, pesticide, decide. What do they all have in common? They all have the suffix "cide" which translates to kill, to destroy, to remove…to cut off.

When you make a decision, you cut off any potential of going back to your pre-decision stage—*that is where your real power lies.*

If, for example, you decide today to become better at closing or to excel at presenting, your goal is guaranteed if you *cut off* any possibility of not developing these skills. That is to say, you now *have to* develop those skills which weren't previously a decision but merely *wishful thinking*. The finality of your decision ensures a successful outcome.

Remember:
If you want
to achieve
anything,
be a Hernán
Cortés and
burn the
boats!

Insight 34

The Power of Love

When the film *The Passion of Christ* came out, my local church hired the local cinema for the congregation to watch it. I remember being shocked by the ghastly nature of the portrayal of Jesus' death. I thought to myself at the time, "what's so passionate about this?" It then dawned on me that Jesus had such a passion for humanity that he gladly chose to lay down his life in such a gruesome and demeaning manner. The interesting thing is that this act of passion affected the world and Christianity grew accordingly.

The point here is that to influence people, you do have to be technically aware, and you do have demonstrate certain skills such as questioning, building rapport, presenting and closing, but nothing mesmerises people like *passion*. Being passionate about what you do, what you sell, your company, your offering, your methods, and about the customer and their business are what really get people to buy.

Passion is not something you learn—it is something you *choose!* Yet the underlying platform of passion is *love*.

Choose to fall in love with what you do and two powerful things will happen:

- You will become more disciplined and willing to deal with the tough aspects of rainmaking.

- People will say yes more to your passion and your conviction, than to just your technical skills and abilities.

Remember:
Passion
begets
passion!

Insight 35

The Parable of the Rainmaker

You can learn how to be a *good* Rainmaker by going to sales training seminars, studying books on sales, practising what you have learned and modelling other Rainmakers around you. However, making that intimate connection with individuals who have come before you and achieved great things can turn you into a *great* Rainmaker. This process is simple: *Read and study the biographies of those you deem your heroes.*

Little inspires one more than when one has read a good biography (particularly an autobiography in the first person). It's amazing how the power of print (or the tablet screen) can make you emotionally go through the same experiences, pain of setbacks, joy of successes and all the drama that the author went through. You get an insight into how the individual thinks, what motivated him or her and where they found their strength.

For me, when I read other people's stories, I cannot help but make comparisons with my own life and road to success. I start to view my quest for excellence through the lens of the literary experience I am going through. The connections made can be profound and inspiring.

The interesting thing is that the biography does not have to be of an entrepreneur or a business leader. One can receive as many powerful lessons from sports personalities, great historical figures and, dare I say, *some* celebrities.

Dr Stephen Covey, in his book *The Seven Habits of Highly Effective People,* highlights an important point: Begin with the end in mind. By reading about other individuals' experiences, your mind begins to focus on what your own biography would be like, and what individuals would say about your life, works and achievements. By thinking about these things *now*, you can begin to sow the seeds of how your destiny will unfold *then* so that whether or not you ever write a biography, your accomplishments will be clear.

Remember: The end justifies the means.

Insight 36

When is the Best Time to Stop?

We all love the *"finger lickin' good"* chicken taste produced by KFC. The story behind the man behind the brand is also interesting. At the age of 65, Harland David Sanders' restaurant and motel had failed. He had known some success previously, so much so that he was given the honorary title of "Kentucky Colonel" by the state of Kentucky for his contribution to the state cuisine. All that didn't matter now because at this point, Sanders took in his first social security cheque of $105.00.

Sanders had nothing else but a chicken recipe of 11 herbs and spices. He decided to go around to restaurants and sell his "recipe franchise". The pitch was simple: "Coat your chicken with my herbs and spices and you will have so much more business. We therefore split the profits".

Can you imagine what restaurant owners' reactions would be? "C'mon! I have my own chicken recipe and it's tasty enough, thank you!"

Sanders' secret weapon was that he utterly believed in his recipe and his proposal, and pressed on from one town to another, from one state to another until he eventually reached South Salt Lake in Utah over 1,600 miles away from where he started. There he met a guy called Pete Harman who finally took him up on his offer and the rest is history.

Try and guess how many rejections he had to his proposal before he got his first yes…? **1,009!** That's right, ONE THOUSAND AND NINE NOs before his first YES. Who reading this would have stopped at 50 rejections, or 600 rejections or even 1000 rejections? Colonel Sanders, in his 60s, believed in his product and offering so strongly that he would have kept going regardless of the number of rejections. It then took his first YES to *change everything*. The franchise operation grew very quickly after that to become what it is today.

It's important to understand that the simple basics such as *belief, persistence, the right pitch, positive mental attitude, fortitude of mind* and *discipline* will always accelerate you to success whatever you do.

> # Remember:
> # Rainmakers
> # don't stop
> # because they
> # can't stop.

Insight 37

The Metamorphic Individual

We all know how successful Will "The Fresh Prince" Smith is. The kid from Philadelphia whose films to date have grossed over $6.6 billion globally. The only star ever to have starred in eight consecutive films that have opened up in America at the number one box office spot.

There are several keys to Will's success: self-belief, long-range planning, laser-sharp focus, determination, persistence, spotting and embracing change, humility, conquering fear and grabbing luck. There is another factor that I believe is critical to Will's success. This is the same power that took him from being a rapper in the 1980s, to an American sitcom star in the 1990s, to a critically acclaimed Hollywood star in the 2000s, and then a successful film producer this decade. That thing is called *self-reinvention*.

Look around you; those that self-reinvent possess staying power at the top. People like Madonna, Clint Eastwood, Sir Richard Branson and Peter the Great, or companies such as Apple, IBM, Virgin and American Express; all harness the power of self-reinvention.

Why is this skill so important? Because one cannot stand still in an ever-changing world. The problem isn't that our environment is changing. It is the *speed* of that change that is dangerous for the static. Manageable constant change is dead and buried. Exponential and unpredictable change is the order of the day and is here to stay.

Recent history is littered with people and organisations caught unconsciously napping - Wesley Snipes got caught out by Will Smith, Nokia got caught out by Apple, Microsoft got caught out by Google and the list goes on. The speed in which your competition can leave you out in the cold can be frightening.

For Rainmakers to *stay* Rainmakers, they have to keep their finger on the pulse of change and not only use self-reinvention to adapt to change but to be at the forefront of change, which creates competitive advantage. The American entertainer Henry Rollins put it aptly when he said: "I believe that one defines oneself by reinvention. To not be like your parents. To not be like your friends. To be yourself. To cut yourself out of stone".

To be the best is one thing; to stay the best requires you to see your business environment and indeed the world through the lens of change and consistently make the necessary adjustments to your skill sets, your knowledge, your type of clientele, your outlook, your tools and your goals. By doing this you will begin to jump from one level of excellence to the next and we know what accompanies excellence…right?

> Remember: Ask yourself: Am I doing the right thing in the right place at the right time to be where I need to be?

Insight 38

Brain Gain

We know that if we want to be fit and full of energy to deal with the challenges of the Rainmaker we must be conscious of what we eat and exercise regularly. Yet the vast majority of what we as Rainmakers do is related to the brain. We need to keep sharp, remember broad complex concepts and very fine technical detail almost simultaneously, make clear decisions, deal with stress and prolonged intense activity as well as face a constant requirement to learn. So why not also exercise our brain muscles?

In the 2009 book *The Sharp Brain's Guide To Brain Fitness*, we are told: "Brain fitness is our brain's ability to readily create additional connections between neurons, and even to promote new neurons in certain parts of the brain. Research in neuropsychology and neuroscience shows that vigorous mental activity can lead to good brain fitness, which in turn, translates into a sharper memory, faster processing of information, better attention, and other improved cognitive skills".

Our profession embodies Napoleon Hill's philosophy in *Think and Grow Rich*. We need to constantly be thinking clearly and effectively to make money, so it's important to keep our brains consistently firing on all cylinders.

Here are a few ideas to consider:

- A healthy body is a healthy mind. Watch what you eat and exercise regularly.

- Tease your brain constantly with crosswords, online brain training, Sudoku, etc.

- Read a random Wikipedia article daily....in fact, just read *anything and everything* constantly.

- Constantly communicate like a teacher, especially to yourself.

- Write instead of type when you can.

- Never use a calculator unless you really have to.

- Daily visualise yourself having *achieved* your goals.

- From time to time, relax and think of absolutely nothing for 30 minutes.

Your most important tool is your brain. Keep it fit and sharp and you will be a much more effective sales professional.

> # Remember: Be a brain bodybuilder and your brain will build you a body of wealth.

Insight 39

Experiencing Time Versus the Experience of Time

Question: What is the difference between a salesperson with ten years of experience and a Rainmaker with ten years of experience?

The Rainmaker has a full ten years of making mistakes and learning from **each** mistake made—thus, by the tenth year his/her wealth of experience would have grown *exponentially*. Others, however, make mistakes over and over again and after ten years they wonder why they haven't tasted real success. One year's experience times ten doesn't constitute ten years of real experience.

It is said that wisdom is experience plus reflection. This is the exact point. You can only gain true experience if you reflect deeply on every wrong decision, unwise move and lost deal. You can learn from anything, including advice from others, your training and personal development.

Your experience *is* your personal and professional equity. That is the value you add to your customers, your company and ultimately your bank balance.

Stop periodically and think about the professional journey you are taking so that it'll be worth it.

Remember:
Good
judgment
comes from
experience,
and
experience
comes from
bad judgment.

Insight 40

Sshhh!! Quiet

Years ago, I stumbled upon an obscure motivational book. The first five or six pages claimed how by doing a very simple thing you could change your life around, achieve everything you ever dreamed of, be full of happiness, etc. Impatiently I ploughed on through the pages looking for the magic solution, the silver bullet. Eventually the answer came: *devote yourself to regular quiet time where you do and think of absolutely nothing.*

At the time, I thought the statement was an outrageous claim, bordering on the point of fraudulent, so I discarded the book. Now, many years later however, I realise that there is something in that claim. What is important to the Rainmaker is clear thinking. Clarity of thought produces excellent output. The hallmark of the Rainmaker is *seeing the immediate beyond the immediate*: the ability to focus consistently on the details at hand *and* see the effects much further down the line. In other words, being tactical and strategic simultaneously. It is very difficult to be that way with all the fire fighting, crisis management, constant demands on your time, deadlines and information overload.

By adopting a regular habit of spending time stripping your mind of the clutter that builds up you will find that thinking clearly and strategically will come more naturally.

Here is an idea:

- Take some time out in a quiet room where you will not be disturbed for the next 90 minutes or so (early morning or weekends tend to work best).

- Sit on the floor (this prevents you from falling asleep).

- Close your eyes so that you are not distracted.

- The conscious mind has to focus on *something*, so concentrate on your breathing. Listen to it, imagine it.

- To start with, your mind will be all over the place, thinking of all sorts of things.

- Do nothing else. Just sit there. Initially this will be difficult to do, but like anything new, repetition will help you through the initial stages.

- After about 20-30 minutes, your mind will settle and relax. Enjoy it for another 20-30 minutes. Don't let your mind wander. Focus on your breathing.

- Once you are truly relaxed, start to think of important things, like your goals or important decisions you have to make of which you are unsure.

- Ideas, answers, convictions, understanding and appreciation all come to you when you are in state.

Monks have meditated all over the world for centuries, but it seems now more than ever, with the pressures we are all under and the rate of change we deal with daily, that quiet time is needed to help us achieve. It is yet another tool in the Rainmaker's toolbox. Try it.

Remember:
By coming
face to face
with the
moment,
you open up
all sorts of
possibilities.

Insight 41

A (Physical) Moving, Stirring, Agitation...

We like to think that the quality of our decisions is purely based on rational thought: one weighs up the pros and cons and comes to a perfect conclusion with complete ease and skill. In reality, this is rare. What really governs our actions and reactions to our environment is *how we feel*. Our emotions govern how we feel. We all need to use our brain to think and learn, but the Rainmaker also recognises the power of his own emotions and those of others and develops the skill of self and relationship management to get results. This is emotional intelligence.

Jack Welch, former chairman and CEO of GE once told the Wall Street Journal: "A leader's intelligence has to have a strong emotional component. He/she has to have high levels of self-awareness, maturity and self-control. He/she must be able to withstand the heat, handle setbacks and when those lucky moments arise, enjoy success with equal parts of joy and humility. No doubt, emotional intelligence is rarer than book smarts, but my experience says it is actually more important in the making of a leader. You just can't ignore it".

Several studies around the world demonstrate a clear correlation between a higher emotional intelligence and sales performance. These studies show that the business realities we operate in today cannot sustain those individuals that simply hard sell their way into accounts. These individuals also manage to hard sell their way out of the accounts since they are not able to deal with constant setbacks and feelings of failure.

Rainmakers are able to understand the emotional content of their thoughts, decisions and actions. To ignore how to understand and manage your feelings is to play Russian roulette with your targets and ultimately your career. The game of selling is full of setbacks, self-doubt, backstabbing by others, prospects' double-dealing and many other disappointments. Maintaining self-control and fortitude of mind is not something that just *happens*, it is a process requiring self-awareness and personal development over time but the rewards are life and career enhancing. The same goes for helping and managing the emotions of others you interact with— prospects, customers, management, suppliers, your colleagues. Understanding that we are all emotional animals will allow you to get the best out of all these relationships.

Research emotional intelligence, assess your own EI quotient, learn to develop it and begin to use it as another advantage towards sales success.

> # Remember: Don't be emotional over people's emotions and yours. Simply use its power to move ahead.

Insight 42

They're Not Just for Biting...

My tailor at Rosen & Nathan is nicknamed Smiler. Each time I have an appointment with him I am reminded of that fact. He just can't stop smiling. It is not a grinning type of smile, but a nice warm smile that exudes confidence and trust and although you never see him when he is not smiling, you never really get sick and tired of his smile—though I sometimes wonder whether *he* gets sick of smiling.

In Dale Carnegie's 1936 bestselling book *How to Win Friends and Influence People*, a whole section is dedicated to the power of the smile. Dale wrote, "Your smile is a messenger of your good will. Your smile brightens the lives of all who see it. To someone who has seen a dozen people frown, scowl or turn their faces away, your smile is like the sun breaking through the clouds".

The beginning of a successful sales process is likeability through rapport. Without the prospects liking you from the start, it can forever be an uphill climb. Showing a genuine interest in your customers, clients, prospects and associates is critical to building rapport, yet the only initial outward expression of this is your facial expression and body language. A warm and genuine smile creates an impact. It does all the messaging to the client for you. A smile sells you before *you* sell you. A smile tells the prospect: *This person truly wants to help me.*

Make no mistake about this, I am not advocating going

everywhere with a ridiculous grin on your face and expect orders to fly your way. A smile should simply be an outward expression of an inward harmonic chorus of warmth, self-confidence, trust and a genuine interest. The smile is the *conduit* that transfers these elements to the recipient.

It is not just teeth that make the infectious smile. It's the facial expression, the eyes, the air you give off and the body language. All these factors are embodied to provide the smile that endears the prospect to you time and time again. Dale also stated in his book, "Charles Schwab told me his smile had been worth a million dollars. And he was probably understating the truth. For Schwab's personality, his charm, his ability to make people like him, were almost wholly responsible for his extraordinary success".

You can't really learn or practise a warm smile. A smile is the representation of a state of mind which you need to *remember* possessing every time you meet someone. The more you remember to think positively about who you are and what you are as well as how you can make a difference with someone *every day*, the more you will remember to truly smile into the lives of all who come in contact with you.

> # Remember: Likeability equals stickability.

Insight 43

Diamond Life

Pressure. It seems to be a constant companion. A friend that spurs you on or a foe that gets you down, depending on its mood. Pressure is something that will never leave us as Rainmakers. Why should it? With it coming from management, other colleagues, the competition, customers and mostly *ourselves*, all we can do is appreciate it, understand it and manage it.

There are two aspects to pressure. There is the type of pressure we take in as described above. There is also the kind of pressure we can sometimes give out to our prospects when we get frustrated that things are not moving as we think or hope they would.

Lord Sebastian Coe once said, "All pressure is self-inflicted. It's what you make of it or how you let it rub off on you". Therein lies the key. A little bit of pressure when times are OK is manageable and only helps keep you motivated. When times are tough though, if you allow it, pressure can debilitate you and limit your output. Like a true professional, always prepare for the worst-case scenario. Try and imagine how you would positively handle real pressure when times are hard, *before* times get difficult. This mental preparation will serve you well.

Your clients are also under pressure and if their timetable somehow conflicts with yours, putting them under pressure will not accelerate things but may even hamper the relationship you spent so long developing. Learn to let the pressure *flow* through you with no resistance like a gentle breeze—that way you will always have a clear head to deal with the unexpected twists and turns a Rainmaker always comes up against.

> Remember: Pressure can give power as well as take it. Choose to be empowered.

Insight 44

The Rainmaker's Guide to...

Experience is the mother of wisdom. Experience teaches. Experience moulds the professional. Experience creates a better Rainmaker. All this we know and appreciate. Without our ability to learn from our experiences, we will never grow professionally. Lack of growth in this regard costs value to your clients and will cost you money.

So we know we have to use experience to grow. But, how do we find the positive in the mistakes we make through our initial naiveté? How can we capture the essence of our experiences as and when they happen to enable our accelerated learning?

My answer is straightforward: *Develop an Experience Journal.*

Yes, a journal. Like the captain's Log that Kirk, Picard, Sisko, Janeway and Archer of *Star Trek* would write, depending on the starship and stardate!

Most of the time, when we make a wrong decision or follow the wrong process, we end up experiencing the ramifications of that mistake. We mull over the set of events in our minds again and again until our minds move on to something else. Our minds do have the capacity to learn from that episode simply by thinking about it, but the *learning experience* is rather limited and, many a time, negative. Why? Well firstly, the mind has a way of being emotional about *everything*—it's very difficult for rationality to feature in the replay of the black and white horror or the drama movie that signifies the experience. Secondly, once the replay *moves* to your subconscious, the mind gets busy with other things and thus you *forget*. This simply increases the possibility of making the same mistake again in some shape or form.

Writing your experiences down on paper, however, completely arrests the irrationality process of your mind. Your words on paper form a new powerful learning encounter, particularly if you also write down *what you have learnt* from the error of your ways. The beauty of an experience journal is that you can relive the positive learning episode again and again, which can only serve to precipitate and reinforce your growth as a Rainmaker.

Do it today. Buy an A5 notebook and take it everywhere. Write down your mistakes, insights, understandings, revelations and corresponding goals. Let this be *your very own Rainmakers Guide to...*

> # Remember: Your journal makes your journey on the road to success a lot smoother.

Insight 45

There is No Substitute

Bill found himself in a sticky situation. He was smart, really smart, but for the industry he was in, being smart was not a big deal. It rained smart people in the IT industry. Bill knew that in order to make it, he'll have to work hard, and he did. Bill stopped sleeping, stopped changing clothes. All Bill did was code, code and code. If he wasn't coding, Bill was working out ways to out-manoeuvre the competition. He worked and worked and worked until he broke through and people stopped calling him Bill and began to refer to him as Mr Gates!

Nothing really beats simple hard work. Yes, you can work smarter, you can be skilful, you can learn the tricks of the trade, you can be good with people, but nothing can substitute *unadulterated hard work*.

You have thought through and written down your work goals such as: what will you bring in? Who will you target? How will you over-achieve on your targets? You know what skills you want to develop to aid you in achieving these goals. All that's left is to get down and *do it*. It takes hard work to really get things done in a sustainable manner that produces consistent output.

Hard work is the "stuff" that glues everything you have learned—skills and experiences—together. According to the former British prime minister, Margaret Thatcher, "I do not know anyone who has got to the top without hard work. That is the recipe".

Focus on what you need to do. Ignore distractions. Control your thoughts and stick to the plan. Find the essence of what it is to work really hard, uninterrupted, throughout the year and I guarantee you will over-achieve on your targets!

Remember:
The better
you get;
the easier
hard work
becomes.

Insight 46

Love the High

Sales is a game. It therefore needs to be played. To be played well, you need to *enjoy* it.

Enjoying what you do makes a huge difference to the process and thus the outcome. Yes, it's true you need to be serious about selling, deadly serious, but you can thoroughly enjoy the seriousness of the game.

Successful athletes, sportspeople, musicians, actors, entrepreneurs and all sorts of professionals enjoy the fundamentals of the games they play. They focus on the buzz that favourable results give them. The anticipation of that "high" gets them through the difficult lows and even the repetitive boring bits as they know once everything comes together and happens the way it should, it's great, just great.

That's exactly how it is with our profession—Rainmaking. If you can't enjoy what you do, irrespective of what is happening around you; if you can't work smart and hard for the buzz of closing the deal, developing opportunities, fostering relationships and growing accounts from acorns to oak trees; then you're simply not in the right profession.

Remember:
Love your
profession and
your profession
will love and take
care of you and
yours.

Part Two

The Rainmaker's Practice

"It always seems impossible until it's done".

Nelson Mandela

Insight 47

So...What Do You Do?

Is selling a true profession or just another set of potential moneymaking activities? Average salespeople think the latter and Rainmakers *know* the former. In truth, selling is whatever you want it to be and whatever you make of it. People look down on selling because of the antics of non-professionals attempting to play the sales professional, but in reality, the men and women who take pride in selling and do it well are largely responsible for the economics of the world.

John Patterson, owner of NCR and the mentor of IBM's Thomas Watson once said: "Nothing ever happens until someone first sells something". When you really reflect on that statement, nothing actually does happen until a sale has been made in any industry worldwide. No sale, no development—economic, financial or social; be it regional, national or global.

HRH Prince Philip, Duke of Edinburgh once wrote: "Some people seem to believe that governments can create employment by waving some magic wand, but no manufacturing enterprise can survive if it cannot profitably sell its products, which means that employment depends on profitable sales".

These statements remind me of the bees of this world. The world as we know it would truly end if honeybees suddenly stopped being bees. Their contribution to the sustainability of the ecosystem is beyond imagination. Why? Because bees are professional pollinators as we are professional economic pollinators.

The profession of selling has been around for thousands of years, from the bazaars in Middle Persia to the merchants of the Renaissance; from the pre-war Swiss bankers to the power brokers of Silicon Valley. Those that sell—and sell well—change the world.

To be a Rainmaker, one must be a professional. To be a professional one must seek to excel at one's profession. To do that, one must respect the profession, learn from it and contribute to it.

Remember:
Your
Profession
is only as
noble as your
attitude and
intent towards
it.

Insight 48

Selling Vs Selling

I once sat next to the CEO of a geotechnical consulting firm on a flight. As we reached cruising altitude, I began to use the opportunity to conduct some last minute preparations for the meeting I was to have with my prospect on landing. He must have peered over and looked at my prep notes because he asked me, "So you're in sales then?" I told him I was. He then said, "I guess it all comes down to personality and price then?"

I looked up, smiled and replied, *"Yes if you're selling energy utilities door to door!"*

Most people associate selling with high activity, fast-talking and order taking where personality and price is what wins the day. The reality is that this is indeed true...*for a certain type of sale.* What most people do not realise is that there is selling and there is selling. Different environments require different selling methodologies, which in turn require different selling skills and in many cases, a different type of sales professional.

Neil Rackham and John R. DeVincentis in their 1999 book *Rethinking the Sales Force* assert three typical but very different sales environments: Transactional, Consultative and Enterprise. Each has their styles of selling and each have their rightful place in the business environment. Each also has their Rainmakers.

Rackham asserts that in transactional selling, customers know exactly what they want. Because the product or service required is widely available and commoditised, price is normally the value driver. Buying cycles are short and the sales process is characterised by high activity.

Furthermore, consultative selling is based around more complex solutions for problems that are more difficult for the customer to grasp. Price more often takes a back seat to getting the solution right. The buying cycle is longer. The salesperson is therefore a solution provider through adding value.

Finally, enterprise selling is based on collaborating. It is more of a case of selling the idea that two companies come together to add mutual value. The buying cycles can take even longer, with the salesperson being an innovator and understanding how to integrate companies.

Though there are numerous sales methodologies out there, these are the three broad types. The problem arises when salespeople do not understand the skills required to be successful in their environment. They can, for example display transactional selling skills in the consultative sales arena with disastrous consequences. Rainmakers know what they sell and *how* they should sell it.

Know your customer, know your company, know your industry but most of all, know your required sales methodology and develop the right skillsets.

> # Remember: It's not just what you sell that counts, it's the way it's sold.

Insight 49

Trait Pick and Mix

Your personality is the culmination of all the genetic and environmental factors you have been exposed to. It is the outward expression of who you are to the world. Your personality is unique to you. The question has been posed to me many times: "Do I have the right personality for sales?" or the statement: "I'm not your typical salesperson, therefore I'm unsure as to whether I can perform as such". This in turn begs the question: Is there a particular type of person that will succeed in sales? The answer is yes. There *is* a type of person that will achieve in sales. That person is the Rainmaker. The Rainmaker, however, is not defined by a *type* of personality. They can be personality types like introvert or extrovert. In fact, the Myers-Briggs Personality Indicator identifies 16 different personality types, ALL of which can be successful as a Rainmaker.

To really make it in this game, it's the *traits* that matter. Traits can be defined as habitual patterns of behaviour, thought and emotions. Psychologists tend to agree that there are typically five big traits (also known as the five factor model) that we all display: openness, conscientiousness, extraversion, agreeability and neuroticism. It is the combination of how we manifest varying degrees of these traits that determines our outcomes in any endeavour we take on.

A 2008 study by Adrian Furnham and Carl Fudge of University College London compared the personality and sales performance of 66 sales consultants from a large organisation and came up with a different combination of traits. Their research showed that those who displayed *Conscientiousness* to their profession and *Openness* to learning achieved the most success, regardless of their personality. By definition, these traits can be brought to the fore whilst other traits such as neuroticism and extraversion can remain in the background simply by understanding yourself and being dedicated to fashioning the right patterns of behaviour to achieve success. *Whoever you are,* you can be that successful sales professional. Just be yourself and develop the Rainmaker in you.

> Remember: Nature and nurture may make you, but it's you who makes the Rainmaker.

Insight 50

Ready?

I see today's sales professional as "the last boy scout". As a scout in my younger years, I had to embody such qualities as discipline, honesty, integrity and fair play.

We all know the Scout Motto: *Be Prepared!* Well, here's what Baron Robert Baden-Powell had to say about that phrase:

"The Scout Motto is: BE PREPARED, which means you are always in a state of readiness in mind and body to do your duty".

My question to you today is: Are you always in a *state of readiness*?

I cannot overstate the importance of being prepared, being ready, being set. The Rainmakers out there seem to know what to say, how to say it and when to say it. They seem to know what decisions to make and when, and most importantly, they seem to be consistently *ready*. It's not down to luck, or spontaneity—no, it's down to constant, rigorous and intense preparation on their part, thus luck and spontaneity are a natural result of their efforts.

Before you go to that meeting, prepare.
Before you pick up that phone, prepare.
Before you make that presentation, prepare.
Before you coach your insider, prepare.
Before you enter into negotiations, prepare.
Always be in a state of readiness.

Prepare for everything, strive to understand everything beforehand and success will surely be yours.

> # Remember:
> # The 5Ps:
> # Poor Preparation
> # Precedes
> # Poor Performance.

Insight 51

It's Like Learning to Ride a Bike...

To become a Rainmaker, you need to master all of the required skills that will form your armoury. If you are serious about becoming the best, about living the life of a Rainmaker, you have to identify all the components of your profession, that is all the tools you will need to succeed *and you must master them.*

So, can learning these required skills really be like learning how to ride a bike?

Let us break the "riding a bike" learning experience down, shall we?

OK, stabilisers off! You jump on the bike and you start as if everything is cool. You're thinking, "if I can do this with the stabilisers on, without them should be a doddle". You immediately fall off and hurt yourself. You somehow tentatively get back on the saddle, but this time you realise it's not that simple and you take it easy, really easy. With practice you realise you can do it, and as you eventually ride through the park, you are still aware of what you should and shouldn't be doing. Eventually, after many practice sessions, you start to ride without even thinking about it and you're a master rider at last!

The process you went through (all those years ago, I'm sure) is called the four stages of learning, initially proposed by Abraham Maslow. They are:

- **Unconscious Incompetence:** *You don't know that you don't know how.*

- **Conscious Incompetence:** *You realise that you don't know how.*
- **Conscious Competence:** *You constantly have to think how.*

- **Unconscious Competence:** *You've mastered how and you do it without thinking.*

This is the process you *have* to go through to develop a new skill. If you recognise this and know what stage you are at any one time in the learning of a skill, *you will accelerate the process.*

Identify the Rainmaking skills such as researching, prospecting, qualifying, questioning, building rapport, presenting, pre-closing, closing, asking for referrals, conducting meetings, handling objections, etc.

Wilfully go through the four steps to master these skills one by one. Make this your primary goal for this year.

> Remember: Mastering a skill turns a thought into a gift. Success is found in presenting that gift to the world.

Insight 52

The Salespreneur

Andrea Jung, former CEO and Chairman of the $10 billion a year Avon Products Inc. is quoted as having said: "You have to combine instinct with a good business **acumen.** You just can't be creative, and you just can't be analytical".

There is only so much you can sell and so far that you can go if you limit your mind and activities to just selling. What makes you more than a salesperson, what makes you a Rainmaker, is the development of an instinct—an acumen—for the wider view of the business landscape.

Consider the difference between the territory and the map. If you are on the ground and you look around you, what you see is the *territory*. If you are way up in the air looking down at the same landscape, what you are observing is the *map*.

It's not enough to simply have a territorial view (and thus attitude, actions and expectations) of your work, job, career etc. You must also establish a panoramic view of the map of doing business.

Gone are the days of IBM-type sales executives calling on predetermined prospects and customers *touting* for business with a silver tongue and a ready pen. The world is different now, more adventurous, requiring a range of technical, selling and business skills. A good instinct and a strong business acumen are paramount if you want to get and stay ahead.

Here are some ideas to reflect on:

- Think like an entrepreneur.
- It's your business so run it like yours.
- Learn from the best, research and read the biographies of other business giants.
- Take a wider view of the industry, markets and the economy.
- Subscribe to business dailies and weeklies like the Economist, FT, Inc., Fortune, etc.
- Find new ways to target prospects.
- *Top Tip* read Innovation and Entrepreneurship by Peter F. Drucker.
- View your job beyond the 9 to 5 paradigm. One gets rich outside those hours.
- Manage yourself and others, including colleagues, partners and customers.
- Develop instincts for new opportunities, regardless of how different the idea may be.

Life is entirely about cause and effect through choices. Thus, it's up to you to choose what you really want to do and how you want to do it. But if you are serious about becoming a Rainmaker and want to drastically increase your income, you have to undergo a major shift in your thinking, decisions and actions and start to become more self-starting, self-generating and entrepreneurial.

> # Remember: Selling is never enough in the business of selling.

Insight 53

Death of a Salesperson

The salesperson is dead! You sell, yes, but you are not a salesperson. So what are you? You are a *Problem Solver!*

Organisations buy because they are desperate to solve problems, avoid potential problems or attain a goal. Be it cash flow, profit, productivity, efficiency, competitiveness, staff morale, customer service, systems availability, downsizing, growth or any other problem, Rainmakers help their customers uncover these problems and demonstrate how they are best placed to help *solve* them.

Companies are never static; the day static begins to creep in is the day the company starts to die. They have to constantly flow with (or sometimes against) the tide of innovation, change, competitiveness and customer needs. Through this constant motion come corporate and departmental problems desperate to be solved in which Rainmakers quickly rise to the position of trusted adviser and agent of positive change.

The traditional skill of selling forms only a small part of the process. Getting the prospect to understand where they currently are and how the solution a Rainmaker offers is the right fit and then making it all happen, *that is the process.* This requires a multitude of skills.

Always think about the typical problems your customers may knowingly (or unknowingly) have. Think of how your company can help put your customer or prospect in a better position than they are already in. Then make it happen.

> Remember: It all starts with problems. Position yourself correctly to solve them and you'll gain the right reputation.

Insight 54

"Mr Rainmaker, Your Attitude Precedes You"

What is every prospect's biggest fear when you first encounter them?

Making the wrong decision? Well not exactly. That's the second biggest fear. The answer is simple. You!

You are by far the biggest fear they would have when they first encounter you either by phone or face-to-face. Why? Because *nobody likes to be sold to.* Everyone loves buying, be it with their own money or company funds, but no one wants to have the feeling of being "pressured" into a buying decision. *Buyer's remorse* is that painful period after one has been pressurised into making the wrong purchase. It's the memory of buyer's remorse that keeps prospects afraid, distrustful and resistant to salespeople like you.

So how does a Rainmaker help put the prospect quickly at ease? Simple. By *never coming across as a salesman.* From the first instant, Rainmakers come across as an expert in their field that simply wants to add value to the prospect straight away.

I don't believe that it has to take years to get to become a "trusted advisor" to a customer. If, in your mind, you see yourself as the prospect's trusted advisor from the very start, then that's how the prospect will receive you. If you straightaway build a rapport with the client, discuss their needs *together*, show them a roadmap of how YOU can work with them to resolve their challenges and keep firmly to your promises, then not only will you and your company benefit from the *lifetime value* of that client but referrals will also be abound.

> Remember: The "trusted advisor" status is merely a state of mind.

Insight 55

The DIY Professional

Anytime one mentions studying or being a student, one conjures images of college, university or an academic course of some sort.

What do Lewis Hamilton, David Beckham, Richard Branson, Helen Mirren, Tom Jones, Ridley Scott, JK Rowling, Stephen Hawking and Margaret Thatcher all have in common? Yes, they are all successful, yes, they are all wealthy and yes, the Queen has honoured them all in some way. But what really sets them apart from others is the fact that they are all lifelong students of their professions—their crafts, if you like.

To be a true professional in your industry, to truly take what you do seriously, you've got to have the discipline and deep commitment to become a student, a disciple of that trade. Everything about what you do has to flow in your veins always.

To be a Rainmaker, you have to know everything about *what* you sell and everything about *how* you sell it. You must consistently commit your own time, energy and money to learning, to studying, to understanding, to *knowing*. And because nothing ever stands still, studying should never stop.

Study your industry. Study your competitors. Study your product and service portfolio. Study your target markets. Study your client's organisations and your clients themselves.

Study your company's strengths and weaknesses. Study your sales process and techniques. Study trends in technology that may affect your clients. Study changes in business practices that may also affect your clients. Study new and innovative methods of consultative selling. Study other successful Rainmakers in other industries. Study, study and study…always. Never stop studying!

> Remember: The trusted adviser who is not in the know cannot advise and cannot be trusted.

Insight 56

The Whole Perspective

There is always a great inner civil war waging within salespeople—something that we all struggle with from time to time. It is also the same thing that forms one of the differences between a mere salesperson and a true Rainmaker. What is this inner challenge?

It is the battle between knowing our limits when making promises to the customer and the desire to make as much commission as possible out of a deal.

Just as a Tibetan monk progresses through levels of enlightenment, sales professionals have to journey through certain developmental stages and this conflict, which arises from a narrow focus on just the commission cheque, forms part of the lower rungs of the path to Rainmaker edification.

The 1970 book by American sociologist Dr. Edward C. Banfield entitled *The Unheavenly City,* referred to earlier in *The View From the Hubble,* depicts the culmination of extensive research into what made people and projects successful. The book's conclusion: *A long time perspective.* Banfield found that the further into the future one's priorities were based on, the more chance one would achieve success.

That principle definitely applies here. The cause of that inner civil war is *short-termism.* The Rainmaker always considers the *lifetime value* of the customer when doing business with them. Therefore, they never promise something they will have trouble delivering.

It's important that we understand what the boundaries of our products, services, company and even ourselves are. Knowing this will allow us to make our intentions clear with our clients.

> # Remember: Take the long view with the customer and they'll take the long view with you.

Insight 57

Fresh Thinking Required

Dr Stephen Covey's *The Seven Habits of Highly Effective People* has sold over 25 million copies in 40 different languages since it was first published in 1989. It's a life-changing book and I thoroughly recommend it. Of all the seven habits, the first Dr Covey presented was the habit of being *proactive*.

All successful people are proactive. They are not afraid to use their own initiative and make decisions. In the complex, multidisciplinary world of selling, this habit is crucial, especially in today's difficult business environment.

Out of the habit of being proactive comes innovation—new ways of doing things, fresh methods of achieving results, smarter techniques of turning prospects into lifelong customers.

Always ask yourself:

- Is there a better, smarter, quicker, sharper, more cost-effective, more professional, more enjoyable, more profitable way of doing this?
- How can I better make use of my time?
- How can I add value to my prospects and clients?
- How can I interact better with different departments?

Remember: It's the few proactive ones that make the world progressive whilst the rest simply take advantage of that progress—
where do you fall?

Insight 58

The Oracle

We all want to be that all-round Rainmaker. That professional who immediately and implicitly understands customers, who always knows the questions to ask and the answers to give. That polished individual who possesses not just the detailed technical knowledge but also the uncanny ability to discuss many issues related and unrelated to their speciality. How does one balance the studying of all this information with a lack of time to spend actually burying one's head in a mound of technical books?

The answer lies in *trade magazines*. Yes, the lowly and often neglected trade and industry publications. OK, so they are not much to look at when examined at face value. However, the consistent and religious absorption of their contents over a substantial period can completely transform your professional life.

The news, articles and opinions written in the pages of these publications are by industry experts and practitioners. They are generously sharing their wealth of product, technical and industry knowledge for next to nothing. Rainmakers take advantage of this, in print and online, to enrich their understanding of both the buying and selling sides of their industry, including the interconnectivity with other industries.

In 1159, the English author, educationalist, diplomat and Bishop of Chartres John of Salisbury, wrote in his Metalogicon, "Bernard of Chartres used to say that we are like dwarfs on the shoulders of giants, so that we can see more than they, and things at a greater distance, not by virtue of any sharpness of sight on our part, or any physical distinction, but because we are carried high and raised up by their giant size".

The point here is simple: using the knowledge of others can elevate you and your professional career, and industry magazines are the quickest and most convenient means of achieving this.

Start subscribing to and sticking with industry publications today and become the all-round solutions consultant your customers are demanding and praying for you to be.

> # Remember: Consult with the oracle and you will soon become the oracle.

Insight 59

Mr Nice Guy Always Wins...Right?

Building rapport with the key players in the prospective account is vital to the success of the sales process. We often cite the old sales adage *people buy people* to illustrate this point. Sadly, too many salespeople misunderstand what building rapport really means, often to their detriment.

When I first started in sales, I remember this particularly large deal I worked hard to close. I did everything I thought was right. The main decision-maker and the influencers all got on with me like a house on fire. Our price was competitive, our solution exact. However, I lost the deal to a competitor. I was devastated. I simply could not understand where I went wrong. I turned to my mentor, David, for advice. We sat down for half an hour discussing what had happened. Finally, David asked, "Did you start and build a strong rapport with them?"

I looked at him, somewhat bewildered. "Of course, I did. I've just told you we all got on so well, we're all like mates".

David smiled wryly. "Mates, huh? Do you know what building rapport really means?" Before I could eagerly answer the question, David quickly interjected: "Listen carefully, there are only two things that rapport has to produce in your prospects: *trust and confidence.* That's it. You can be jolly mates all you want, but if they cannot trust you and have the utmost confidence in you, our solutions and this company, then kiss any profitable deal bye bye!" Later, I learned that the feedback from the prospect was also the same.

Like with most selling skills, building rapport is not about the hope that you will get on with your prospects through the sheer force of your personality. That may be where it ends, but it all starts with technique not personality. Five powerful techniques to build rapport worth studying and practising in are the following:

- **Reciprocity:** Add real but *free* value to the prospect early in the sales process so that they feel the need to work closer with you further into the deal.

- **Commonality:** Quickly finding areas you both have in common (professionally and personally) but without making it too obvious or over the top.

- **Mirroring:** Neuro-linguistic programming (NLP) provides methods of mirroring certain traits in prospects so that eventually they naturally feel they can relate to you.

- **Character:** You say what you do and you do what you say.

- **Professionalism:** Constantly maintaining an air of professionalism through actions of integrity and knowledge.

Think about these ideas, research them, practise them and perfect them. Trust and confidence are the watchwords here. Your goal is to be in a position where clients always want to deal with you and only you.

> Remember: Mr Nice Guy is always the runner-up
> to the trusted Rainmaker.

Insight 60

Clever, Very Clever...

I sometimes love to immerse myself in those gripping suspense thriller novels where my heart's constantly in my mouth, I'm at the very edge of my sofa and I'm wondering, *"how in the world will he get out of this one?"* Towards the end, things start to unfold and the main character triumphs and you go, *"Ah, I see. Clever, very clever".* You realise that the hero of the book had a strategy all along.

When one mentions strategy, military generals, business leaders and chess masters spring to mind. However, Rainmakers have to be shrewd strategists. Why? Simple. Where there is a prize and there are competitors, in order to win, there *has* to be a strategy. Without strategy, one simply reacts to *everything*: your fears, other people and circumstance. One starts performing haphazard tactics with little results. The great military strategist Sun Tzu put it succinctly when he wrote: *"Tactics without strategy is the noise before defeat".* Rainmakers never do anything that is not aligned to a particular results-orientated strategy.

What exactly is strategy? Strategy is simply a *plan of action* to achieve a particular goal. This definition implies that strategy needs to be developed and re-developed at different stages of your sales process. Say, for example, during the prospecting stage you may use a numbers game cold calling strategy to generate leads, or a referral strategy, or a networking strategy. Once that is decided, you will then decide on the tactics you will employ in line with the strategy to achieve your aim. You may, for example, have a plan of action to penetrate a particular account by gathering information from the lower rung of the organisation before tackling the more senior decision-makers or vice versa. Rainmakers have a strategy for everything, yet it is not obvious. Sun Tzu also wrote, "All men can see these tactics whereby I conquer, but what none can see is the strategy out of which victory is evolved". The best strategists are those that the competitor cannot see coming.

Strategy is about thought. Tactics is about action. You need time to develop and evaluate the options open to you at every stage of the sale. Consult others that are more experienced than you are. Formulate a strategy. This can be revised at any time as circumstance dictates, but at least you have a plan of action. Just having and following carefully crafted strategies increases your success rate exponentially. Read books on sales and business strategy, in order to understand how to select a strategy. Be the Rainmaker that your competitors will constantly say: "*Ah, I see. Clever, very clever*".

> # Remember: Thought precedes strategy, which precedes action, which precedes success.

Insight 61

The Queen's Gambit

Don't you just love those movies where the hero has anticipated every move of the villain? Even when it looks like everything is going wrong, the hero has it all sussed. That's why I love watching Tom Cruise's *Mission Impossible* movie franchise.

Now imagine YOU are able to *anticipate* every move your customer makes, every question they ask, every objection they make, and every tactic your competitors make within a given campaign. Would you make better decisions? Would you be more confident of a better outcome?

As Rainmakers, we can go a long way to achieving that skill. You know what you sell and how you sell it. The way to anticipate is to take the time out and really *put yourself in the customer's (or competitor's) shoes*. Ask yourself questions like:

- What objections would I pose to this product/service?
- What would be my motivations to wanting to buy?
- What would I say if I was merely "tyre-kicking"?
- If I was a competitor, what would I do at this stage?

By using your imagination to be in their situation, second-guessing them can become an art form.

Remember: If
you are always
one step ahead,
you can have
more control of
the outcome.

Insight 62

The Practice

A man walks up to an elderly lady in London and asks her, "How do you get to the Royal Albert Hall?" The lady replies, "Practice, young man, practice".

An old joke, but it does highlight something crucial in the Rainmaker's playbook. The willingness to practise for the rest of one's life.

The Cambridge Handbook of Expertise and Expert Performance, published in 2006, highlights practice as one of the main determinants of being a champion and not natural talent.

David Beckham was one of the greatest scorers using set pieces in the history of soccer. The way Beckham would "bend" the shot and land the ball in the back of the net was legendary. What was also legendary was the way he practised. He was known to always be the first on the training ground and would leave hours after everyone else. Beckham, like Michael Jordan, would spend his professional life practising and practising and practising. There was no 'until'. They just kept on practising.

Selling is about developing and using a particular set of skills. The more one hones these skills the better the results will be. Rainmakers practise everything. They practise prospecting, conversations, storytelling, asking questions, presenting, negotiating, writing—the list goes on. They practise, alone, in the mirror, on their family, friends, colleagues, in real life situations. Whenever the opportunity presents itself, they practise. Rainmakers never stop practising *no matter how good they get.*

Without developing life-changing and life-enhancing habits and regularly sharpening them, you will simply be performing critical sales tasks on a wing and a prayer and that never produces consistent, high-performing results. Practise today and every day.

> # Remember:
> # There is no glory
> # in practice, but
> # without practice,
> # there is simply no
> # glory.

Insight 63

Elegance Needs No Adornment

Leadership isn't about management. Some of us are managers but if you want to be successful at this job, this profession, this vocation, you need to display leadership—*elegant leadership*.

Everyone responds to leaders. This phenomenon occurs in the vast majority of human interactions. To me, leadership is about being responsible for your actions, being true to yourself, being courageous to follow your path, working proactively with others and striving for *true excellence* in your chosen profession.

Elegant leadership, however is all of the above but with a unique charm that can captivate others, cultivating an attraction that compels people to respond to you and your ways.

This concept is critical when selling into larger corporate accounts. As a Rainmaker, you are a leader of your *own business* within your firm's business. You manage yourself, your accounts and your business. Your managers are there to support you but you have to lead the way. If you act like a leader in everything you do, you will certainly become one and your clients and prospects will respond to you favourably.

Remember: You either lead or you follow. Followers, however, always become runners-up to deals that have only one prize.

Insight 64

Amongst Equals

I remember six weeks into my sales career, my mentor David accompanied me to my first meeting with a prospect. Though I had been to meetings with David in the past, they were his prospects and he had controlled the meetings. This meeting was for my very first prospect and David was there to act as a silent observer.

The meeting took just over an hour. I felt I handled things rather well. David, true to his word, stayed completely silent through our engagement, only speaking to exchange pleasantries before and after the meeting.

Later that day, David and I sat for a coffee to discuss the meeting. "Jonas, how do you think that went?" David asked, his face expressionless.

"I thought it went really well. I feel I asked the right questions, he responded with honest answers and I think we've come away with a number of concerns we can help them with," I replied, smiling and feeling elated.

David smiled. He had this look on his face as if to say "you'll learn…eventually".

I didn't like that. "Why does this guy always have to burst my bubble?" I remember asking myself, my jaw tightening.

"Look, Jonas, you did a cracking job in there…" my jaw loosened slightly. "…However, you're already going to have a real uphill battle on your hands getting the deal".

The joints in my jaws almost snapped. I had to really put myself together and muster the question, "Why do you say that, David?"

David paused. "You did a really good job getting this meeting with a senior person in the company, but the way you spoke, the questions you asked, the points you put across and your body language convinced the prospect that you'll *never* be his equal. You lacked parity and without parity, you have no leverage. Without leverage it'll always be difficult to hold your ground and work with him to get the deal done".

I learned a painful but powerful lesson that day. Building rapport with prospects and customers is important, but rapport without real mutual respect is a misaligned relationship. Though salespeople are already on the back foot because of the negative reputation caused by the few, Rainmakers make it clear respectfully they are to be taken seriously and their time and resources are just as valuable as the prospect's. This will come across in how you set the conversation, the way you speak, what you say, the intelligent and powerful questions you ask your body language, as well as using every opportunity to display real character and integrity.

This is not about being aggressive or difficult, this is simply about possessing the mind-set that you are a valued professional who is only willing to present value to those who recognise that.

Be true to who you are, know your capabilities, invest in your confidence equity.

> Remember: Relationships win deals. The question remains: is it a relationship of equals or that of servitude?

Insight 65

Newton's Universal Law

I remember the first time I met a former boss of mine; he had a presence when he walked in the room. Yes, he owned and ran a £1.5 billion-a-year group of companies, but on meeting him, you got the sense that he had always possessed this *thing* about him. My former boss, like all Rainmakers, possesses gravitas.

Morgan Freeman once said, *"I gravitate towards gravitas"*. I think Morgan was expressing what people already naturally do. By sheer definition, someone or something with gravitas *attracts*. Rainmakers cannot make rain without attracting the clouds that produce rain—the customers.

Some people say gravitas is charisma. That is true to an extent. I, however, believe that charisma alone is not gravitas. In fact, many misunderstand the sales profession because many salespeople have all the charisma and charm but little substance. To me, gravitas is charisma, character, experience and a highly developed sense of self-assuredness all in one package. People can sense it immediately they come across it and they become attracted to it because it is both inspiring and aspiring and everyone wants to be part of that. Prospects and customers always want to work with people who display genuine gravitas. It is a tool in the Rainmaker's arsenal that none of us can do without.

Is gravitas a product of nature or nurture? Are you born with it or do you have to develop it? I believe it is both! We have locked away in our DNA the ability to manifest the kind of presence gravitas can create—we just have to develop the four areas: charisma, character, experience and self-assuredness. It is a propagating cycle: the more *true* experience and understanding you immerse yourself in, the more your character is shaped and the easier it is to understand people and develop charismatic qualities. As you heighten these qualities you begin to develop more self-belief and self-appreciation. Then something just happens and everything falls into place and everyone else can see it, feel it and sense it.

A word of caution, however: one cannot *fake* gravitas. If you have not gone through the process above and you start to put on a display of what you *think* is gravitas, nobody will feel it, but only *see* arrogance and self-importance, which, of course, has the exact opposite effect.

Rainmakers learn to develop from within. They know that every experience shapes them, moulds them and builds them to the point where they develop something which is not just a skill, but a gift very few have, which everyone gravitates towards.

> Remember: Develop the true essence of your professionalism and soon everyone will know it and gravitate towards it.

Insight 66

The Sacred Truth

On March 30, 1901 during a business speech in New York, Mark Twain said "Honesty is the best policy..." I think this is a profound statement which should be the cornerstone of our professional lives.

The selling profession has an image problem. It always has. One of the main issues is that salespeople are seen as dishonest and lacking *integrity*.

We hear the word integrity banded about as if it is something to pick up. Rainmaking however is about influencing people to do business with you and nothing positively influences people more than when you demonstrate *genuine* integrity.

So what does integrity actually mean? Well, it comes from the Greek word integritas which simply means whole.

Whole? Yes, in other words, complete. You are who you are and you should remain who you are. You should always strive to be better but you should stay true to you. The only way you can do that is to be completely honest with *yourself* as well as others.

The Rainmaker exudes integrity through being open and honest about who they are and how they conduct business with others. Mark Twain's full quotation was actually: "Honesty is the best policy...where there is money in it!"

Remember:
Say what you
do and do what
you say and
your will earn
the lifelong
trust of others.

Insight 67

Time. The Academic Construct

Everyone has something to say about time management. In the 80s it was the filofax, in the 90s it was the electronic organiser. There are a million and one seminars on it, over 100 million results when you Google it, and Amazon stocks over 31,000 books on the subject, yet the typical sales professional still seems to not be able to get everything they need done, when they need it done in the way it should be done.

Of all the time management "methodologies" I have read, the simplest and most effective method for me comes from Brian Tracy. He dubbed it the ABCDE method.

Every morning (or the evening before), make a list of what needs to be done that day. Prioritise them into ABCDE.

A: The things that have to be done, because they are urgent *and* strategically important (complete these first).

B: The things you could do but the cost of *not* doing them is minimal (only do these after you have completed *all* that is on the A list).

C: The things that you like to do but there is zero cost to not doing this activity (do these after and only after you have completed *all* that is on the B list).

D: Stands for *Delegate*. If you can delegate this task, then do so. You can't and shouldn't attempt to do everything—that is what teamwork is about.

E: You should think of things that you do in a day that you should not be doing and *eliminate* them from your day as they serve only to limit your day in every way.

I would add one more to Brian Tracy's methodology.

F: Find organisations and other people to *outsource* jobs to. In today's connected world, there are many ways administrative tasks can be outsourced to other professionals all over the world without even meeting them. This is the rise of the "gig economy". Tasks are uploaded and subsequently downloaded in complete form for a relatively insignificant fee. This frees up the Rainmaker to make the real money.

Remember, you cannot *manage* time; you can and should only manage *yourself* and the base unit of yourself, relative to time, is the *task*. It is doing the right tasks at the right time that is a catalyst to Rainmaking success.

Warren Buffet once told a group of eager Harvard students that the key to success is *output!* The more productive you are in a particular endeavour, the more valuable and, thus, successful you would become.

> Remember: Your output is the
> realisation of your goals.

Insight 68

You Are the Product!

You know, what sets the Rainmaker apart from the rest is *value*. Sounds like a cliché, doesn't it? Everyone talks about adding value here, value added there. But let's think about this from the customer's perspective for a second:

There are numerous other companies like yours, all purporting to do exactly what your company does, in the same way and more often at the same price. The smart customer has to make a decision to go with one of you. How will they make that decision? What will be the real differentiator? Where will the real value come from?

In a scenario like that, there is only one value source: YOU!

In the current business environment, it's not enough for the sales professional to have to communicate value, one has to *embody value*. In real terms, that's getting to a point with the customer where they trust you implicitly. They rely on you; they know inherently that you have their interests at heart.

The only way to be in that position, the position of *trusted advisor* is yes, to understand your product, your solutions, your company and your industry, but it is also critical to understand and appreciate the customer's issues, company, marketplace, strategy, politics, people, aspirations (personal and corporate), their own customers, and most of all, the customer's problems.

Remember:
You are Rainmaking
when the customer
needs to work with
you because of you,

Insight 69

Defining Value

Many years ago, my mentor and I went to see a customer about a project they were considering. David took the lead in the meeting. I remember him introducing me as his "associate" and then urging me to take the meeting notes. Grudgingly, I complied, muttering to myself "if he needed a secretary he should have hired one". After the meeting, we grabbed a coffee and began to review the notes. David asked me to list the areas I felt the customer needed help with, areas we could add real value. I listed seven areas.

David shook his head, smiling. I remember thinking how I used to hate it when he did that. "There are only four areas important to the client", David quietly said.

"Well, I'm sure it was seven areas," I retorted, becoming slightly irritable at this point.

David looked me dead in the eyes, paused for a couple of seconds and slowly asked, "Who determines value?"

I responded, "The customer".

"Bingo", smiled David. "The customer was clear on the four areas and categorically *stated* them. Regarding the other three, you made an *assumption* that they were important to the customer, but ultimately that'll almost be double your focus for half the requirement".

The lesson here is that though we know our products and services, and what value they can add, we cannot interpret value; only the customer can. Every time I go into a new business opportunity, I empty my mind of any assumptions or illusions about what the customer requires. I ask and ask and ask until the customer explicitly states what is important to them for that particular deal. I will then focus all my energies in demonstrating how my company and I can meet those needs. I also rank the requirements in order of importance and focus accordingly.

Rainmakers know that value is a moving target. Value is dynamic and totally depends on the customer, the company and the deal on the table.

> # Remember:
> # Only the
> # customer can
> # define value...

Insight 70

The Value of Co-Creation

The title of the MBA dissertation I wrote was *"Is Key Account Management Paramount to Unlocking Value in Business Relationships?"* The question delves into issues around value exchange in large accounts where both the vendor and the customer form a "dyad" and together develop and exchange value.

Ok, so the above does sound like a load of business jargon, but the real question here is, *"is value creation just the preserve of the Rainmaker, or can the customer get in on the action too?"* The phrase that pops out here is value co-creation. Rainmakers recognise that real and long lasting relationships are formed when customers directly participate in determining, designing and implementing their solution.

This is a powerful lesson I learned from my old mentor, David. His words still ring in my ear, *"If you form an equal partnership with your client from the very beginning they will never leave you"*.

The old paradigm of - customer has a problem, you have the solution, customer pays for the solution, you provide the solution and the problem goes away – is fading fast and is being relegated to the smaller transactional sale. In the larger, complex selling environment, if the sales process and buying process are merged into one and the Rainmaker and the prospect work together as equals to understand what is happening and how solutions can be reached, the dyad formed will be impenetrable.

Remember:
Empower your
customers,
co-create!

Insight 71

Rainmaker is My Name and Disruption is My Game

Five! That's the number of industries master Rainmaker Steve Jobs transformed over the course of his life. *Five.* The worlds of personal computing, animation, music, phones and mobile computing are all different today because of Steve Jobs' influence. Sir Richard Branson, Jack Welch, Elon Musk, Jack Ma and Larry Page, like Steve Jobs, are all disruptive Rainmakers using vision and innovation to challenge the status quo of doing business and to create new forms of value.

I knew a Rainmaker who, in 2007, sold computer equipment to mid-sized companies. By accident, this Rainmaker found out she had a higher success rate if she held the first couple of meetings with first-time prospects on the phone and then only met them face-to-face later in the buying process. She invested in a well-known virtual meeting software and started holding many of her meetings from her home office. She added value to her clients through convenience and allowing them the space to build trust with her and her solutions before the physical meeting. This small innovation was the single act that trebled her revenue and doubled her profits within a year.

Selling is the one area where methodologies and techniques don't change as quickly as the rest of the world does. This is great news for Rainmakers as it provides them with opportunities to *think and do different* than competitors and to create new ways of delivering value to customers.

But being a disruptive Rainmaker is about more than innovating when finding customers. Disrupting the way buyers think about their solutions is one of the pillars of Rainmaking. Rainmakers are not afraid to challenge the status quo. They show the customer new ways of thinking about problems, processes and even goals. They develop and articulate deeply powerful questions that enable prospects and customers to think outside their paradigm, thereby showing them the sense in innovating.

You know your industry, you know your solutions, you've seen hundreds of customers innovate and solve business problems, right? Why not package all that experience and exposure and help your prospects innovate too?

> # Remember: Rainmakers disrupt by innovating and planting the seed of innovation in their customers.

Insight 72

The Scientific Artist

There is a definite science to making rain. However, buried within the science of selling is the art form. As we know, science is about rules, a specific process that provides set outcomes. Art, on the other hand is about creative expression, about testing the boundaries of what is deemed possible. It's about dealing with the random and unpredictable in theatre.

Every sales trainer will tell you there are a number of basic key stages the typical sales process goes through:

- Prospecting
- First contact
- Need qualification
- Cover the bases
- Develop & present proposal
- Dealing with objections and negotiating
- Gain commitment
- Implementation
- Referrals/account management

Knowing what stage you are in at any time will serve you well as each stage requires a set of skills to create a successful result. That's the science.

The only problem is that, in reality, the syntax of the sales process is completely dependent on the customer's drivers and timing. For example, you may find a situation where the customer is ready to commit immediately, or, like snakes and ladders, you go through the steps, only to find that you have to start all over again with no guarantees with another steering committee. In theatre, the science of it all may simply go out of the window and your sales artistic flare is needed.

Ray Kroc, the original force behind the $25 billion McDonald's Corporation, once stated, "The definition of salesmanship is the gentle art of letting the customer have it *your way*".

Every Rainmaker knows that the fundamentals of selling form the science, the techniques, the principles; but being able to discern complex changes in the customer's situation and instinctive use those changes to form desired outcomes *is* the art of selling.

> # Remember:
> # Master the
> # science,
> # practise the
> # art.

Insight 73

ExQ

When you ask a salesperson, "Why do you do what you do?" the inevitable response will be, "I'm in it for the money". Now there is nothing wrong with that response per se. It's just that if you are solely in it for the cash, when all is said and done, when the money is earned and spent and industries rise and fall, what would you be left with?

If you ask the same question to a successful Rainmaker, the answer would be along the lines of: *"I'm in pursuit of excellence and its associated dividends"*. Rainmakers knows deep down that if they persistently search for the achievement of excellence in whatever they do, the wealth will naturally follow *but* it will be accompanied by a whole lot more: a sense of achievement, great business friends, fun, real experience, an incredible lifestyle and as Abraham Maslow put it, the attainment of self-actualisation.

Success and happiness! Isn't that the point of life, of work? The beauty of the selling profession is that it can give you all that, if only to pursue excellence with fervour and dedication.

Here are my three tips regarding pursuing excellence:

- Break down what you do into compartments such as researching, cold calling, building rapport, managing meetings, asking powerful questions, presenting, handling objections, closing, asking for referrals etc., and strive to be excellent at these skills. Also look at yourself as a whole, how you project yourself, what your work ethic and attitude is like, and strive to be better—to *excel*.

- Study others. The great business guru Warren G. Bennis once said: "Excellence is a better teacher than mediocrity. The lessons of the ordinary are everywhere. Truly profound and original insights are to be found only in studying the exemplary". The fastest way to be better is to model others who are already better. Read about the success stories of others, study them, learn from them and apply the same principles in your own quest for success.

- Be honest to yourself! If there is an area in your profession you need to be better at, focus on it, chase the "excellence quotient (ExQ) in that area, and don't stop until you achieve it.

Pursuing excellence is a lifelong endeavour. It never stops. The great thing is, once you start enjoying the benefits of excellence, you will never ever want to stop chasing it. That's the stuff of life.

> Remember: The spot where you finally catch up with excellence is where you will discover the Rainmaker in you.

Insight 74

Your Most Prized Possession

Hip hop culture uses many phrases to define certain issues and distinguish what is important to that way of life. One phrase that sticks out and which is taken very seriously, is *"Word is Bond"*.

The phrase emerged from the street gangs. Violence and thuggery may be part of street culture in urban America, but a code of ethics is critical to the organised chaos of the street.

Word is Bond exists in every facet of society, from factory workers to the bourgeoisie, from the military to the ruling class. Making a promise or an agreement and adhering to it is how business deals are sealed.

In selling, *Word is Bond* should be at the forefront of your dealings with your prospect. Always stick to your promise, *no matter how small*. Don't under-promise then try and over-deliver, just promise and make it happen.

> Remember: Keeping to your word is the beginning of forming a bond with your customer!

Insight 75

The Eigth Wonder

The first TED video I ever watched was by mathematical scientist and journalist Dr Adrián Paenza. Dr Paenza theorised that if one had enough paper that was 0.001cm thick, it would only take forty-two (yes, 42) folds for the height of the "theoretical paper" to span just under 250,000 miles, which is about the distance to the moon. Think about that for a second: 42 folds to be high enough to reach the moon. That is the power of exponential growth. That is the power of *compounding*.

The power of compounding can be seen everywhere. In nature, in the right conditions, animal and plant populations grow at an astonishing rate. Throughout history, under the right conditions, industries and business grow exponentially in ways that sometimes dumbfound spectators.

Rainmakers know the secret. It is simple. The Rainmaker will design a formula, a system of achieving, and work that system steadily over and over again until the system starts to grow arms and legs of its own. That unique system will start to work for the Rainmaker. The world famous motivational speaker Jim Rohn said, "Success is nothing more than a few simple disciplines, practised every day". Your system could be the way you prospect, or the way you manage your time or the type of deals you go for. The key to unlocking the power of compounding is time and consistency. Einstein once said, "Compound interest is the eighth wonder of the world. He, who understands it, earns it. He, who doesn't, pays it".

It's the "interest", which is the methodology you develop and use, that will over time, work for you and produce dividends that will be out of this world.

Remember: Develop
the right habits
and methodologies
slowly but surely
and allow the power
of compounding to
flourish.

Insight 76

The Power of Negative Thinking

The former British prime minister, Harold Macmillan will be remembered for many things including finally ending the British National Service, giving swathes of sub-Saharan Africa independence, rebuilding the special relationship with the US after the Suez Canal crisis, as well as the *Vassal* and *Profumo* Cold War-related scandals. His famous quotation however, is timeless. When asked what represented the greatest challenge for a statesman, Macmillan replied, *"Events, my dear boy, events"*.

Macmillan knew that for a politician to think he or she has everything sussed is foolish. It was the sequence of events triggered by 911 that provided President George W. Bush with his greatest challenge. It was the Iraq War that provided former British prime minister, Tony Blair with his greatest challenge as did "Brexit" for another former British prime minister, David Cameron. Like time and tide, a crisis waits for no man.

The Rainmaker is fully aware that there are forces beyond his control and at times beyond the Rainmaker's knowledge or comprehension. Anything can happen that might change the course or direction of the sales process at any time: new business drivers, new decision-makers, internal politics, a merger or takeover, market forces or plain old apathy. In reality, there could be a thousand and one changes in the prospect's world that can immediately (or slowly and silently) redefine the landscape of the deal that has been carefully crafted for so long.

All one can do is react. The best form of reaction, however, is *proactive reaction*. The only way you can proactively react to situations is to start by *thinking negatively.* Sounds counter intuitive doesn't it? Just imagine however, you sat down and analysed all the various things that could go wrong with a particular deal and how you would best manage the situation, *and then* prepared yourself and your contacts for such potential outcomes.

By being acutely aware of all possible eventualities, the Rainmaker knows how to respond to situations and achieve the best results, even if it means knowing when to confidently walk away from a deal or even an order. Granted, all this takes experience, but this also takes an inquisitive and imaginative mind regardless of prior experience. Besides, experience starts today.

Always think about your deals, where you are, where you're going, what could go wrong, and how you would still guide the deal to its desired conclusion.

> Remember: Either you define circumstance or circumstance will define you.

Insight 77

The Teacher and The Imparter

There are a number of avenues to learning concepts and developing skills. These avenues can include reading, studying, experiencing, discussing, modelling, repeating and reflecting. However, one of the most effective ways of getting things to sink in quickly is by *teaching*.

Steven Covey, in his 2004 book *The 8ᵗʰ Habit*, contends that the passage to greatness can be found through forming this habit: *Find your voice and inspire others to find theirs.*

No man is an island. As humans, nothing really happens if we don't interact in some form. Interaction, by definition, works both ways. The benefits are symbiotic. What I mean by this is simple: If you learn something for the first time and you "teach" your experience to a colleague, not only will your colleague benefit from a learning experience, but *your own learning* experience will be even deeper, *plus* your relationship with your colleague will be enhanced. This is all positive. This is growth.

An experience shared, taught and discussed will only form a greater experience for all involved. Start today to have the mind-set to constantly profess your knowledge, experiences and understandings to others, as this in turn will heighten your own awareness and appreciation of it. It's important also to recognise that *how* you teach is proportional to the depth of the overall learning experience. The famous American writer, William Arthur

Ward, once wrote: "The mediocre teacher tells. The good teacher explains. The superior teacher demonstrates. The great teacher inspires". Inspire others and your own inspiration will be twofold. Rainmakers always inspire and are always inspired.

Remember:
The teacher
becomes
the taught.
The imparter
becomes the
great.

Insight 78

It's Neither a Metaphor Nor a Simile!

I heard a story the other day about a Rainmaker who was trying to close a large deal. She was up against a well-established competitor and they were both at the final stages of the sales process. From the prospect's view, the two companies were indistinguishable. Both companies were invited for a final presentation. During the Rainmaker's presentation, they asked her, "*How would you compare your company to that of your competitor's?*" The Rainmaker's answer was simple. She compared her company to her competition by using comparisons between the prospect's own company and the prospect's main competitor in their industry. This elegant yet powerful analogy enabled her to close the deal.

Communication is everything in the game of sales. The Rainmaker's biggest asset as a value generator is his or her ability to convey concepts, ideas, innovative thoughts and general information in effective yet powerful ways. One of the most persuasive methods of doing this is through analogies—*using another concept similar in structure to drive home the point being made.*

Shakespeare used analogies in his plays. In Act II, Scene 2 of Romeo and Juliet, Juliet said, "a rose by any other name would smell as sweet". Juliet's point was that Romeo's surname, being "Montague", should not make a difference. If a rose were called a "pumpkin", it would still smell sweet; and though Romeo's bore the name of Juliet's family's arch enemy, he was still a great guy.

To be able to use effective analogies in meetings and presentations may appear like it comes naturally to the sharp and witty Rainmaker, but in reality, this is rarely the case. Rainmakers think out ways to express concepts and details *beforehand,* jot them down and practise them in order for them to flow naturally in theatre.

Use analogies when asking qualification questions, use them when breaking down complex technical details to customers you know are not technically aware of that concept, use analogies during presentations and when pitching your company and your solutions. Heighten your most important points with analogies.

Remember: One powerful ten-second analogy is worth more than one hour of needless waffle.

Insight 79

Serendipity

Marilyn Monroe once said, "There is no such thing as chance". I would disagree and I'm sure Monroe took advantage of many chances when they presented themselves. Chance is a mysterious concept. It's everywhere yet it's nowhere. It sometimes presents itself in the most unlikely of areas at the most unlikely of moments.

As humans we are designed to be successful in our pursuits—to be the best we can be is encoded in our DNA, it's in our survival genes. That's why we have the ability to work hard, to think and to plan. But we also have *chance*. Every individual that has triumphed in any endeavour (including Marilyn Monroe) will tell you about a *pivotal* chance encounter that they seized upon. Conversely, every person who has failed will also tell you about the chance encounters not taken that they may regret!

Napoleon Bonaparte is quoted to have said, "Chance is the providence of adventurers". As much as selling is a game, it is also an adventure: every person you meet, every presentation, every deal closed, is the adventure of Rainmaking.

Though chance may be seen as an enigmatic and omnipresent concept, a Rainmaker's job is not to seek to understand it's esoterical dimension but simply to take advantage of it and you can do so in the following ways:

- **Believe**: For chance to exist, you have to believe it does.

- **See:** Train yourself to spot the chance when it presents itself. Look for it in every conversation, every meeting, every phone call and every opportunity.

- **Be ready:** Responding quickly and effectively is crucial to getting the fullness of this mystery. Always prepare yourself for the inevitable "chance encounter".

As Rainmakers, we have to use *every* tool at our disposal to be the best and create business where one may think there *is* no business—the element of chance must be seen as a tool for achieving this.

> Remember: A chance spotted and harnessed becomes an opportunity. Opportunities developed with skill will become business.

Insight 80

Who Finds Who?

Prospecting is really about *that search*. The search for the ultimate customer. Though companies use various marketing initiatives to attract prospects, Rainmakers go out in search of that client. It's a bit like the TV's *The Apprentice*, Lord Sugar knows that he has to endure a lot of pain to get to the ideal candidate. However, he always has an impression in his mind of the kind of apprentice he wants, an impression that he has worked out *beforehand.*

The key to bigger and more profitable deals is to work out the ideal customer beforehand, plan out your search strategy and start looking. It's irrelevant at this stage if they are looking for you. The Rainmaker controls this process by deciding whom she wants to work with and then going about convincing the ideal prospect the same.

I knew a Rainmaker in London once who really wanted a particularly large organisation as an account. He toiled for over four years on the account before getting his first order. By the time that order came, he was on first-name basis with all the relevant senior executives as well as many in middle management. He understood the organisation's strategy and culture and they all trusted that he and his firm would add value to their critical business processes. His first order? Over £25m, and that was in 1999. The account ended up being one of his firm's top five accounts at the time and is still an account for the company almost 20 years later.

The lesson here is that you can be in control of the prospecting process by deciding whom you want to do business with long term and by having the determination and tenacity to make that business yours.

Remember:
The prospector
finds the gold,
not the other
way around.

Insight 81

The Benefit of Mathematics

To be successful at selling, there is only one thing that matters. Every skill or technical ability you strive for only exists to enhance this one thing. This abstract concept is "the numbers".

You have probably heard the phrase "it's a numbers game". Well, that's because it is. When I first started in sales the numbers I lived by were the following: Commissions to invoices to revenue to orders to presentations to proposals to meetings to prospecting phone calls.

I have set this sequence in reverse order to demonstrate the endgame first, and that is to make money. However, the amount of money I made was directly proportional to the amount of calls, meetings, proposals, etc. that I had to do. This process became a formula, which I could tweak to work for me depending on the competitive environment and my level of skill.

The real question you need to ask yourself is *"What numbers do I work with to achieve the endgame?"* This brings us to the question: *"How much money do I want to make?"*

Here is an illustration:

Annual commission before tax: $150,000.00 (endgame)
Revenue needed at, say, 3% commission: $5m
Average order: $500k

Number of required orders: 10

Number of proposals for one order: 5 (total proposals for 10 orders = 50)

Numbers of meetings for one proposal: 3 (total meetings for 50 proposals = 150)

Numbers for calls to get a meeting, including incoming leads: 10 (total calls for 150 meetings = 1500)

To summarise:

1500 calls = 150 meetings = 50 proposals = 10 orders = $5m invoiced revenue = $150k commission

Now this is just an example and YOUR endgame and unique sales ratios (USR) may be different, but how are you going to know how to achieve and exceed your target if you don't know the road map and the ratios?

All the selling and technical skills are there to enhance the ratios by increasing the probabilities. So you may become better at closing so you get 15 orders out of 50 proposals rather than 10, or you might be a better presenter so you get 70 proposals out of 150 meetings, and so on. Inversely, if you are weak in an area you could simply increase the probabilities that you are strong in to enhance your chances further down the "funnel". Always adjust your ratios as they are as live and as dynamic as it gets.

Remember: Use numbers and probabilities to control your endgame or you will be under control of what's out of your control!

Insight 82

The Gold Prospector

Rainmakers are *master cold callers.* There are no two ways about it. One can view cold calling negatively or positively. Most of us see cold calling negatively, both the prospect and the cold caller. Negative words like, nuisance, patronising, confrontational, pressured, dishonest, evasive, repetitive, boring, demoralising, indiscriminate and thankless all come to mind when one considers cold calling. No wonder it is seen as a no-no for both the salesperson and the prospect.

However, consider this, *what other prospecting method can you completely control that can be used to quickly build a powerful pipeline?*

If one imagines the act of cold calling from two different perspectives, the first is an infantry soldier with a machine gun trying to mow down an advancing special forces team and the second is a well-trained and experienced sniper patiently focusing on the right target. Within this war analogy, the latter would undoubtedly experience far more success.

It is the same with cold calling. Telephone prospecting is not going away. It is still the fastest way to cut through and start your business. It is still the most effective way to quickly build or boost one's pipeline. However, the days of picking up the (now not-so-thick) phone book and starting to dial from "A" are well and truly dead.

Of all the marketing initiatives out there, productive cold calling can give a company the best returns because you cannot get a more targeted situation than you speaking directly to the individual who you know has the *money, authority and need.* By speaking to the M.A.N. and you pitching it right, your chance of a successful outcome is very high.

Cold calling puts prospecting and pipeline building firmly in the hands of the Rainmaker. Success from other prospecting methodologies is a bonus. Rainmakers also see it from the perspective of the customer. I have had several of my best clients thank me for taking the time to seek them out and cold call them. Prospects are busy people, and just because they have a particular requirement does not mean they will take the time to seek you out and cold call you!

Here are some ideas to consider:

- View cold calling as a positive legitimate way to build your pipeline.

- Thinking positively about what you are doing will show in your voice and body language, which prospects will pick up.

- Prepare, prepare, prepare. You cannot prepare enough!

- Cold calling can have four positive outcomes: a yes, a re-schedule to call again, a referral to another individual or a call back in the future. There is no negative outcome.

- The essence of a cold call is to seek out the right person/s (the M.A.N.) and to gain an appointment. You are not there to sell your products or services at this stage.

- Focus on AIDA—Attention, Interest, Decision and Action.

- Cold call regularly throughout the year regardless of how your pipeline and targets are doing as business is cyclical and not linear.

- Be ready for any objections.

- Try and enjoy it.

If you want to build a business, you have to build a pipeline. The more you cold-call, the bigger your pipeline will be and thus the more likely you will overachieve on your targets. It really is as simple as that.

> # Remember: Develop your pipeline and it will develop your bank balance.

Insight 83

Enter the Dragon

However good you are or how high-flying a Rainmaker you are becoming, there is always something that follows you everywhere. This is something that will constantly remind you that the business of selling should just be a game.

That chimera is *rejection*. The Chimera was a Greek mythical monster that put fear into the hearts of people. It was a monster, a dragon that needed to be slain. As it was just a mythical figure, it could not be slayed since it lurked in the minds of individuals. However, one can ride this dragon instead.

Rejection is the number one reason why people leave the profession of sales whilst Rainmakers always find a way to move past this mythical fear.

Here are some statistics:

- Nearly 100% of the top 5% of salespeople do not have issues with rejection.

- Nearly 100% of the bottom 74% of salespeople have issues with rejection.

As a concept, rejection is harmless. In real terms, the prospect is not rejecting you; they are simply making a decision. The real battle, where you have to take care, is how you take that decision.

If you take rejection personally, then you have an internal struggle on your hands. If you take rejection for what it is, such as the prospect not being ready or the customer choosing your competitor, then you can use this opportunity to take stock and evaluate your strategy, or simply see it part of the "numbers game" and move on.

It is important to recognise that rejection has just as much a place in our profession as competitiveness, commissions or word is bond!

> # Remember:
> # Reject
> # rejection and
> # not yourself.

Insight 84

The Things We Think But Do Not Say

"…I was remembering even the words of the original sports agent, my mentor, the late great Dickie Fox, who said: 'The key to this business is personal relationships.' Suddenly, it was all pretty clear. The answer was fewer clients…"

I remember watching the scene in the 1996 film *Jerry Maguire*, where the main character, Jerry Maguire, sat in his hotel room in the middle of the night and penned the memo…sorry, the mission statement entitled *The Things We Think but do not Say*".

Question: How many clients, opportunities, accounts and business is enough for one person to keep the attention, focus and drive at its peak state continuously? Only you (or your sales manager) can truly answer that.

Rainmakers focus on the end game and work backwards. The question they ask themselves is not the *number* of clients required but the *type* of clients. They realise that it takes roughly the same amount of time, resources and effort to work with a high-value customer as it does with a lower value one.

Therefore, it makes sense to focus on acquiring and developing business with the few who spend more than with the many who spend less. Just make sure you work the numbers so that your closable pipeline doesn't come up short during prospecting phase.

Remember:
It's in the
few that
much can
be found.

Insight 85

The Role of Titles

LinkedIn is a great social media platform to build your virtual network and develop your brand within the professional world. Salespeople also use it to mine for prospects, particularly if one is targeting an account and need to find out who's who. As usual, the key attributes to initially record are the contact's name and *title*. Many salespeople erroneously believe that the title associated with an individual tells you everything they need to know about the *role* of that individual in the prospective account and possibly within the deal. An assumption turns into an opinion that always seems to stick.

I fell victim to this once. I remember working as a sales support executive for my first mentor David. David summoned me into a sales meeting with Mark, the managing director of the firm. The three of us sat around the glass rimmed solid oak round meeting table in Mark's plush office, the atmosphere seemed elated yet tense.

David turned to me, his face expressionless. "Jonas, we now have an opportunity to take on our competitor's biggest account from them."

"Wow, really?" I whispered, not quite sure what the news actually meant. "That's good news right?"

Mark interjected, "That's great news Jonas. The only thing is we don't know who the players are and that's where you come in."

"Er, Ok, so you need names, titles and contact details right?" I asked, my confidence slowly returning.

"That's right, names, titles, roles and contact details for now and we need this info by tomorrow lunch time." David remarked as he stood up, ready to leave the room.

The next day, David and I sat down. I had everything I thought he asked for. I presented all the relevant contacts I could find in the account through research and cold calling. Once I finished, I was beaming impressed with the job I thought I had done. David remained silent. He didn't look happy at all. My mind began to race, 'what have I missed?' I asked myself.

"It took you over a day to get this information right?" David muttered.

"Yes" I responded, still confident in my work. "It's all there David."

"So how do I know who does what, how they relate to each other and to companies like ours?" He retorted.

I looked perplexed, but I carried on any way, "Their titles tell you that, right?"

David ignored my last question. "I asked for their roles as well as their titles. How can I figure out who to talk to, how to approach them and in what order if I don't know what their roles really are?" David's face relaxed a bit. "Look, finding out who the players are is not about what they do but about who influences who. There is a difference, albeit a subtle one, but it makes all the difference in the world to me."

I found out that day that titles, mean exactly what they are, titles and nothing else. Rainmakers spend their time seeking to understand the roles contacts play and where they fit in the over scheme of the deal.

> Remember: Success comes from influencing the influencer, not the influenced.

Insight 86

Baseball

I must confess, being British, I understand baseball as much as Americans understand cricket. A friend of mine took me to a baseball game in Nebraska recently and I didn't get it. So after a while I just cheered when everyone else cheered. There was one thing that I do remember, however: once the batter hits the ball, he has to run around all bases and back to the home plate. Four bases in total.

Rainmakers are like batters: they have to cover all bases thoroughly to have enough to *sense* the fabric and direction of the deal. Different sales trainers, authors and gurus have various names for these bases (individuals and/or teams) within the prospect's organisation that may be involved in the deal in some shape or form, but essentially they boil down to the following:

- **First Base - The Insider:** The person/s who helps you navigate the prospective account and deal.

- **Second Base - The Plighter:** The person/s who feels the pain if the problem is not sorted.

- **Third Base - The Swayers:** The person/s who influences the deal in some shape or form.

-

- **Fourth Base - The Main M.A.N.:** The person/s (with the Money, Authority and Need) who can make the final decision or at least have power of veto.

Rainmakers tend to "trade up", by starting with the Insider who introduces them to the Plighter who introduces them to the Swayers and who finally introduces them to the Main M.A.N, taking note of the political landscape all along the way. However, it can also be vice versa if you're really good…

Remember:
Cover all
bases and
deliver that
home run.

Insight 87

It's all in the Baking

The main difference between an undergraduate and a postgraduate degree is research. I remember studying for my MBA with a wife and two very young kids whilst managing a sales team. It wasn't the easiest of endeavours. The interesting bit was the research I had to undertake for my dissertation and the analysis of the data that came through, before making sense of it all and putting forward my arguments and conclusions.

Rainmakers know that without proper research on behalf of prospective and existing customers, the value proposed will be half-baked.

I have a friend, a true Rainmaker, called Ralph. In the 1990s, Ralph was selling IT products and services to large corporations. This Rainmaker had been targeting a global insurance company for a while with little success. Once laptops started to become a real business tool, Ralph had an idea. He knew laptops would be a good thing for the insurance company prospect, but he needed to show how real the value was.

Ralph already knew a lot about the prospect's organisation. They had a large sales force around the country. He started to delve further into how the prospect's sales force operated. He found out they would visit clients, fill out forms, and post them back to head office for the forms to be processed. This caused delays due to lost forms and mistakes during data entry performed by low paid staff.

Ralph didn't stop there: he spent two full days in the business school library of the local university researching the industry and their customer preferences. He found out the industry was changing to a telephone and Internet-based model as customers were expecting speedy provision of quotations and policies. Ralph also found out that this particular insurance company valued its sales force and the personal touch they provide and wouldn't want to move away from that model.

Ralph had enough to present a "fully-baked" value proposition that included tangible benefits around saving money, increasing margins, demonstrable return on investment and a way to maintain, if not increase, market share all by getting the sales force to communicate with the HQ processing team in near real-time. Ralph won the account and provided the company with a lot more than laptops.

Sometimes, we have to face up to the fact that customers don't always know what they want or need. Rainmakers sometimes have to go and find out, analyse and put together a value proposition to the right person or team in order to be taken seriously. Get into the habit of research.

> # Remember: There is nothing like having a real story to tell.

Insight 88

The Aggressive Patient

Here are some interesting statistics:

2% of sales are made on the 1st contact with a prospect
3% of sales are made on the 2nd contact with a prospect
5% of sales are made on the 3rd contact with a prospect
10% of sales are made on the 4th contact with a prospect
80% of sales are made on the 5th to 12th contact with a prospect

These statistics are banded around the internet but in fact, they cannot be substantiated. But they do highlight two important words: Persistence and Patience.

You need to persist with your drive into an account, getting to know all the contacts, influencing them and developing the sale. You need to keep on and not stop to the very end. Be smart but persist.

It's important to learn the skill (and develop the habit) of aggressive patience. This is where you will yourself to be completely focused on the strategy and endgame even though you feel like giving up! Developing the large sale is like playing a game of chess—you need to carefully consider your moves and countermoves. It's about strategy. In some cases you can get to *checkmate* quickly or you may have to go for the long play. Either way, aggressive patience helps you maintain a cool head, particularly at the final stages of the deal.

Remember:
Patience and
fortitude
conquer all
things.

Insight 89

The Lead(er) in You

Leads! The very word conjures up both pleasure and pain in many a salesperson. Good leads obtained at an exhibition or industry conference: great! Bad and out-of-date leads passed over by the sales manager or by marketing: not so great.

We all recognise leads are the seeds that, cultivated correctly, can grow to the oak trees that can be our most profitable customers. Rainmakers however, also recognise that if these seeds are to be sown on the pathway to success, then they need to have full control over them—anything else may be a bonus.

Rainmakers have various ways to maintain a steady stream of leads, including customer referrals, partnering with other non-competing companies targeting the same customers in the industry, networking (physical and virtual), thought leadership and targeted direct prospecting (yes, cold calling). All these areas I have written about in this book.

Admit to yourself that if you want a larger pipeline and the ability to smash targets repeatedly, you have to go out there and develop your own leads. You have to create a system whereby your actions on a daily, weekly and monthly basis are providing you with enough leads that will ultimately enable you to beat your targets, based on your unique sales ratios (USR).

Once that happens and you get into a lead-generating groove, everything else will begin to fall into place, you'll be more fulfilled and less stressed about the numbers.

Remember:
Don't judge
each day by
the harvest you
reap but by the
seeds that you
plant.

Insight 90

It's Your Voice!

Rainmakers are constantly made aware that voicemail is the new gatekeeper. Voicemail can be a barrier between you and that prospect, that all-important contact you really need to get hold of and meet. It's the bane of our professional lives, it's what prolongs the sales process, and even possibly costs you the deal as competitors get in first…or is it?

The beauty of voicemail is its dual function. On one hand, it keeps unwanted (and mostly unprofessional) cold callers at bay, but it also provides a platform for the Rainmaker to gain the prospect's *attention* because decision-makers *do* listen to their voicemails.

You can use voicemail as a tool to drive your sales process and here are a few tips to consider:

- Research. Spend time deciding who and why you are calling. Think carefully and clearly about what you will say in both eventualities: the prospect picking up or you reaching their voicemail.

- You don't necessarily need to leave a voicemail on the first try. Attempt to contact the customer at different times of the day, especially early in the morning or after hours, as senior decision-makers are also very hard workers.

- Be persistent. Leave more than one voicemail, not too many, as this can be seen as stalking. If the voicemails are specific enough to the prospect's current goals or needs and are integrated well with emails, the contact should be receptive and respond in some way to you.

- Practise getting your *tone* right. Leave voicemails on your phone and play them back. The trick is to come across as confident, interesting and an experienced senior professional with personal gravitas that likeminded executives can immediately relate to and appreciate.

- Make your first few precious seconds count or the prospect will press the "next message" button.

- Take your time and focus on the message.

- Take heed of the tools you can use to cancel or change the message if you are not happy with it.

The point of your message is not to sell anything, but to raise attention by being intriguing. The prospect should be unsure as to whether this is even a sales call. If you have done your research right and the customer deals with that particular area, chances are they will respond. Once they do call you back out of the blue you have to be prepared to pitch the meeting there and then and that's another story all together.

> Remember: A voicemail is simply sending the prospect your voice via digital mail. Make it count!

Insight 91

Chance Encounter of the Only Kind

I was at an industry awards ceremony recently. During the rather dull speeches, I decided to trot off to the bar for a drink. The bar was full and busy due to only one bar person on duty trying his best to serve 30 tipsy middle-aged men at the same time. I waited patiently as the man in front of me placed his order and collected his drinks. He turned around to leave and I immediately recognised him as the head of a large department of a global company. I smiled and quickly introduced myself saying I had helped two of his industry peers save $X within a year. I asked him for 3 minutes 30 seconds to tell him what I could do for him. He told me I had 3 minutes...

Rainmakers have no illusions who they might run into and where. They know that they have to be on top of their game 24/7. They may receive a random call just before they have to walk into a presentation, they may bump into a high-value prospect in a car park, they may be stuck in an elevator, or even notice a prospect whilst on holiday; the permutations of scenarios are endless.

However, it is more than just catching the prospect at the right moment. What do you say that will have the biggest impact? How do you describe who you and your company are and how you can both add value? How do you pitch so that the call to action is smooth, positive and decisive? How do you do all of this in four minutes or less?

The answer is preparation, practice and internalisation.

Prepare: Design your pitch to include powerful words that grab attention, words like imagine, value, show, you, free, results, proven, opportunity, etc. Then, structure your pitch so the transitions are smooth. I like to start with what I know about the prospect's goal/problem/issue then move onto a case study of an industry peer with a similar issue, then move to why my company was chosen and delivered successfully and then finishing with a call to action (follow-up phone call, meeting or a referral). Then, practise, practise, practise. Practise in the mirror, to your friends and family, to whomever will give you useful critique. Once you have "internalised" the value pitch, you're ready.

Remember:

You never know.

Be ready.

Insight 92

The Real Social Network

My parents sent me to a private boarding school and for the first two years, I hated it. I hated it with a particular passion. Everything was strict—even the way you walked on campus had to be "brisk" or you could face corporal punishment. During the holidays, I would constantly complain to my parents, pleading for a transfer to a local day school, but my petitions fell on deaf ears. There were various reasons my parents cited why I had to continue schooling there—discipline, the school heritage, the academic rigour (which apparently was supposed to be good for me) and my favourite: "it'll turn you into a man" Ha! But there was one reason that did stand out. My Dad took me aside after one of my moaning sessions about the school and said, "Son, the relationships you forge with your classmates and housemates today will sustain you for the rest of your life. They'll end up being the basis of your professional network".

He had a point. My Dad made me realise the importance of a network of friends and colleagues has for one's career, which in sales can translate into one's pipeline.

A good network is about relationships; a great network is about *information*. The beauty about networks is that you can control them and decide what to give and get out of them.

Rainmakers invest time and effort into building a powerful network. Rainmakers also know that the characteristics of a strong network are reciprocity and benevolence. They give into as much as they take out of the network.

One particular technique Rainmakers use to add value to their customers and prospects is to cultivate a network that *includes them*. Chances are your clients and prospects experience similar challenges and require similar solutions to these challenges. Rainmakers provide a platform for them to get to know one another and share notes and learn from each other.

Social norming amongst your customers' peers in a setting influenced by you can be a powerful way to grow your pipeline and thus obliterate your targets. Find ways to grow and maintain your network face-to-face and see where the power of compounding can take you.

Remember: A
network is for Life,
not just for the sale.

Insight 93

The Virtual Social Network

One thing that marks the millennial generation that we all currently find ourselves in is the exponential rate of change. The speed is breath taking. Just as inflation lowers the value of fiat currency over time, I sometimes feel like there is a "time inflationary pressure" that lowers the inherent value of *time* over time. All the things that could take place in a five-year period a decade ago now appear to take place within a year. The way Rainmakers find opportunities and work with customers to achieve desired outcomes is no different.

There was a time when cold calling meant "turning up" at offices and waiting to be "seen" by your prospect, then telephone prospecting took off. Now we are in the midst of the social media revolution. Rainmakers embrace this chance because their customers are doing the same.

The power of social media only reflects the power of information…the very thing that is critical to the success of Rainmakers. Your ability to harness the internet and social media can enable effective prospecting and selling. Here are four things to bear in mind:

1. Numerous studies show that more and more potential buyers and buying organisations are having their decision-making influenced by the internet and social media, particularly at the early buying stages.

2. The Rainmaker's own *personal brand* is becoming increasingly important as many prospects can come across the Rainmaker before the Rainmaker comes across them, so having a strong personal image on social media only serves to make the Rainmaker's prospecting process smoother.

3. Rainmakers know that social media has a habit (good or bad) of leaving a "trail of bread crumbs" on the activities, opinions and sometimes the needs of decision-makers. Rainmakers actively mine this reservoir of information to seek out real and relevant prospects to do business with.

4. Rainmakers share and share alike. Relevant content, ideas, opinion and any information that helps customers and prospects gain something even before the Rainmaker meets them.

By proactively focusing on the highlighted areas above you can massively expand your virtual network and the value and influence you can gain from it.

> Remember: Delve feet first into the world of social media and see just how huge the world is.

Insight 94

Pay It Forward

I have stated several times that the business of selling is just a game. The aim is to win by adding real value to whom you do business with. That may be by way of your company's products and services, but the real edge is by what you—the Rainmaker—bring to the table. But all said and done, it's still a game. The interactions you have with prospects, customers, suppliers, colleagues and other business partners are interactions that hopefully yield profit for your company and commissions for you, but they are still just interactions.

Relationships, on the other hand, are more than just interactions; they can last beyond the life of any business deal and in many cases, not even be part of the original deal!

I have a good friend who is always willing to help any prospect. He is not afraid to say no if the prospect is not right for him, but he always knows someone who *can* help. This Rainmaker possesses a vast array of contacts that he can refer the prospect to, contacts he believes *will* add the value the prospect desires.

Rainmakers are primarily relationship builders. Ethics aside, they do not discriminate with whom they build relationships because they know that they are not only interacting, but are creating interactions between others—they therefore pay it forward. These Rainmakers may not gain anything per interaction, but they gain a whole ecosystem that grows bigger by the day. The bigger the personal ecosystem, like gravity, the more they attract business. This is the quintessence of Rainmaking.

Start today to begin building your own Rainmaker ecosystem. Develop cross-industry and cross-speciality contacts because someone else's customer today may be yours tomorrow. You never know.

> # Remember: As your Rainmaker ecosystem grows linearly, the effects on your bank balance can only grow exponentially.

Insight 95

The Commodification of YOU!

Viva Voce. That very phrase strikes fear into academic students the world over. If you didn't quite make the grade in your dissertation, you may be called up to a panel for an oral examination justifying your original work. Viva Voce is a Latin term and it literally means *"with living voice"*. It essentially depicts the power of the spoken word, particularly when it is transferred from one individual to another. So no wonder it came to be used as a synonym for *word of mouth*.

Matthew Weiner's hugely successful 2007 television series *Mad Men* was inspired by a number of Madison Avenue advertising executives who influenced American society in the 1960s through their creative, innovative, revolutionary and sometimes controversial advertising copies. One of those Mad Men was William Bernbach. Bernbach once said, *"Word of mouth is the best medium of all"*.

When dealing with products that need to reach millions of consumers daily such as fast-moving consumer goods, vast amounts of money are spent on advertising to *alert and remind* consumers of the features of the product. In the larger more complex sale however, word of mouth in the account and within the network of your customer *is* your advertising medium. The beauty of it is that it is free—well, almost free. If it was completely free then everyone would be using it successfully.

Rainmakers are *aware* that everything they say and do, every decision they make and every result they achieve goes in some way to creating the perfect advert of themselves and their companies that will spread via word of mouth. Conversely the ineffective salespeople are *unaware* that everything they say and do, every decision they make and every result they may not achieve goes in some way to creating the worst possible advert of themselves and their companies that will also spread via word of mouth. Either way, Viva Voce takes place. Viva Voce does not discriminate. People do. Time and time again research shows that for every person told of a good experience, three or more people are told of a bad one.

Be aware that you are constantly and silently being judged by your prospects, customers, associates and peers in many ways and if excellence is your hallmark, excellence will also be your advertising copy and people will be your medium.

> # Remember: As people buy people, people also sell people. Let who and what you are be bought and sold by people.

Insight 96

Don Kingism

There is a guy I know. He initially sold leased lines for a well-known telecoms company. He did all the things a sales professional should do, but he felt that it wasn't enough. He was ambitious and he wanted more. He knew, however, that he had hit the limit of what the company could do for him marketing-wise. So he marketed himself in his own way using whatever resources were available to him. He studied the industry inside out and wrote many articles in trade magazines about his findings, he willingly volunteered to speak at company-organised seminars, he became an active member of all relevant business and trade associations and he worked the web by optimising his name on the Google's search results. This guy made sure that his name was known and he was the professional to know. The final analysis is that all his efforts made it *easy* for him to attract clients because prospects felt they could *trust* him even *before* they had met him. Within a short period, this Rainmaker began to bring in the lion's share of the company's revenue and through a reverse takeover, bought the company!

Self-promotion is a skill that is rarely discussed in sales training seminars yet it is crucial to achieving anything *beyond* your normal sales targets. More importantly, self-promotion helps you create and maintain business relationships you could only dream of obtaining in normal circumstances. One of the key differences between salespeople and Rainmakers is self-promotion.

Find ways to get your name out there as the one to really want to do business with. Do what my telecoms friend did: use social networking sites to your benefit, make it a priority that all the industry "bigwigs" know who you are and how you add value, get testimonials from existing business relationships out there. Read books on marketing and branding and simply apply those very same principles to your personal marketing strategies. By being innovative, you will be able to forge relationships that last longer than your career.

> # Remember:
> Excelling in the art of professional self-expression will only aid in promoting you upwards.

Insight 97

Ebb & Flow

If you're like me, you are results-driven. In fact, that's a typical quality most companies look for in a sales professional: "You must be results-orientated…"

We are always concentrating on results, so we constantly bombard ourselves with questions such as:

- Will I hit my target this period?
- How many meetings have I done?
- How many deals will I close this week/month/quarter?
- How many calls can I make?

It's true that having a results-oriented mind helps you focus on achieving those results, but *just* pinpointing purely on the result and the result alone can be somewhat limiting and in some cases, de-motivating. It can make you miss a vital thing: *The Process.*

My suggestion to you is think about being *process-driven*. There is a paradox here: by default, the result *comes from* the process. After all, you don't *do* the result, you execute the process which produces the result as a natural by-product of your efforts. That's exactly why it's important to focus on the process, as it's the workflow that produces the output. The more you "micro-manage" the process, the more predictable the results can be.

Aspire to sharpening up the process of opening accounts, adding value to clients, demonstrating that value to them, spotting opportunities, prospecting for new business, helping clients address their issues, etc., and the results shall surely be in your favour.

Remember: Micro-manage a well-designed set of processes and the results will macro-manage themselves.

Insight 98

Small Bet Gamblers

One of the biggest limitations in your job as a Rainmaker are timewasters.

In Ben Younger's 2000 film, *Boiler Room*, they are referred to as "pikers" (small bet gamblers). I sometimes refer to them as "tyre kickers". Whatever they are called, if you are not sharp, you can spend an awful lot of precious time, money and resource chasing after their pipe dreams to no avail.

Time is the Rainmaker's most precious commodity: they understand that the effective use of time is directly proportional to their bank balance and success in life so they avoid timewasters as much as possible.

Spotting the piker is a skill in itself: part qualification, part testing and part instinct.

Rainmakers never assume anything. They test everyone through questioning prospects in various ways and comparing the answers. They are direct and to the point and gauge the prospect's responses. Rainmakers trust and use their instincts.

Don't let timewasters sap your precious commodity and your energy.

Remember:
Only do
business with
those whom
are willing
and ready to
do business.

Insight 99

Free Thinking

I love sports cars. I particularly love Italian sports cars. I have a couple that I cherish. One warm summer's day, one of my cars broke down. Luckily, I spotted a garage a quarter of a mile away. I reluctantly abandoned my beauty on the roadside and walked over to the mechanic's workshop. Chris, the mechanic, greeted me with a smile. After I explained my dilemma, Chris offered to walk back to the car with me. He inspected the car for a few minutes, found the problem and fixed it there and then. Chris then proceeded to explain the fault and advised me on what to do to prevent the problem from reoccurring. When I asked how much I owed him (mentally preparing myself for a sizeable sum), he replied, smiling, "Nothing. All I ask is that you look after her".

That was 8 years ago. Guess who has been my only mechanic since that day? Chris. The Law of Reciprocity is as old as humanity itself. Whether it's random acts of kindness or helping a prospective customer go some way to achieving goals without first paying for it, Rainmakers know implicitly that genuinely offering something tangible for nothing is a powerful deal enabler. Rainmakers are clear that the objective is not to expect something in return; *quid pro quo* does not always work. The focus should be on fostering a longer-term fruitful relationship by first building trust. The Rainmaker is genuinely interested in helping the new prospect and will do anything in his power to help them achieve *something*.

I am not talking about gimmicks like gifts or product samples. Depending on the industry, a trip to a football game or the races may be expected so everyone would be offering that. The bestselling author Peter Abrahams once stated: "To get from people you have to give a piece of yourself, a real piece that matters". The key is to provide a piece that is rare and yet is able to help the prospect realise a goal or a critical task no matter how small that task is. See it like a "leg up" that brings them closer to an important objective. What is that gem that can make all the difference? I like to call it the *Rainmaker's Value (RV)*. That is, that mixture of knowledge, experience, industry exposure and contacts.

Imagine this: All *your* clients, past and present, are in the same position as your prospects. They perform similar tasks, they have similar professional and organisational goals, they are exposed to the same challenges with their roles and are looking for similar solutions. The beauty is that YOU have a wealth of experience and understanding in solving similar problems. The question is: how can you fuse all this experience and knowledge to create a unique package and present to your prospect free of charge? By giving them advice on how to achieve these things, through showing them how other companies experienced the same issues before using innovation and a different way of thinking to achieve desired outcomes.

If you help a prospect by first presenting something of real tangible value that only you can provide, your prospect will become a customer for life. Use your time to build up your unique combination of knowledge, experience and contacts and be ready to hand that over to your next important prospect.

Remember: Trust can only be achieved by giving people the opportunity to test you first. That opportunity has to come free of charge.

Insight 100

The Customerization of the Prospect

Question: When is a prospect not a prospect? The simple answer is when they become a customer. With Rainmakers, there are no in-betweeners, no failed prospects. If a Rainmaker targets a particular account and after all the research and analysis, the Rainmaker is convinced that particular account would be a perfect prospect— i.e. there is the potential for long-term consistent growth, profit and a good commercial fit—then the Rainmaker will chase that prospect *until* they become a customer.

Rainmakers sometimes take several years to gain a real foothold in a particular account. The trick however isn't about chasing a particular individual—the account is very rarely about an individual—it's about the organisation, including individuals, teams, departments, culture and structure. It's about getting the organisation to view you as a partner. This may take months but many a time it can take years to get to that level. Once you are there, however, the rewards are great. Residual revenue will increase period after period. This strategy is the number one secret of Rainmakers. They penetrate a few of these accounts and keep them growing.

Carefully, very carefully, decide what accounts you need to pursue. Do this by deciding the appropriate level and frequency of revenue and profit your ideal account can give you relative to your target. The account of your choice does not necessarily have to be the biggest blue chip company, just the *right* company. Work on the company from the ground up, targeting every relevant individual within the organisation. Understand the company, their goals, their history, their culture, their customers. Find ways to constantly add value for the key individuals, even if it means simply sending them relevant information that you think can help them in a particular area. Moreover, never ever give up. Once the account is yours, the work has just begun. It actually takes just as much work to maintain a profitable client than to gain one. Develop growth targets for your account and find ways to meet and surpass them constantly.

> # Remember: If your prospect has not turned into a customer, then they were never a prospect in the first place.

Insight 101

Face2Face

A 2006 international survey of 1,500 salespeople from 13 industries conducted by Proudfoot Consulting found that on average, salespeople spend 60% of their time on administrative duties or travel. Add other non-sales-related activities, and the remaining 40% of the workday amounts to limited time with customers. The study revealed that many salespeople spent as little as 15% of their time with clients.

One highly critical concept in the corporate selling arena is *face-time*. This is the amount of time spent physically face-to-face with prospects or customers, relative to performing other tasks. Face-time is all about building rapport, influencing, selling, investigating, presenting and closing. It's difficult (though not impossible) to perform these tasks by proxy.

Performing administrative tasks like writing quotes and proposals, checking and responding to emails and working out solutions with others is all extremely important to the smooth running of your business, but face-time is directly proportional to the level of business, which in turn is directly proportional to your ability to overachieve your targets.

Organise your time to maximise the amount of face-time you can give. Plan your day, week and month with face-time in mind.

> Remember: Deals are won eyeball to eyeball. If you're not there, someone else will be.

Insight 102

Share the Glimpse

Poker players never show their hand before the showdown. However, the Rainmaker knows to *show all* at the very start.

Think of it this way. You know the sales process: the various steps from initial contact to closing the deal. Why not demonstrate and agree on a series of actions and decisions in advance with the prospect at the very first meeting?

Taking the prospect through these steps at the initial meeting is important. However, it's crucial to gain agreement up front that as long as they are satisfied with each of the previous steps that they will be happy to move along to the next step. It's at this stage you can determine how the customer *prefers* the sales process to be.

The process by which the client goes through to make a buying decision is as important *to the customer* as the buying decision itself. Show them what they get to start with and they will begin to trust you. Follow the agreed stages through and they will end up always trusting you.

> Remember: Show your hand at the start and you will end up with a lot more than a Royal Flush.

Insight 103

Master of the Living Room

Salespeople tend to be good at meeting people. However, are they always good at meetings *with* people?

When watching a boxing match, you know that everything happens in the ring. Decade-old feuds are won and lost during those three-minute rounds. All the preparation, training and anticipation happened before the ring time and all the pain, glory and life-changing effects will happen after the ring time. Yet ultimately it is the ring time that matters; it is what justifies the before and determines after. Likewise, the place where deals are won or lost is in the client meeting, in the face-time. One could spend hours preparing meticulously for the sales interview but if this is not managed properly, one could be losing ground to the competition, ground that may not be recoverable further on in the sales process.

The Rainmaker knows that to truly master the art of deal-making one must be the master of the face-time. Just like being on stage, managing meetings is about 90% planning and practice, and 10% delivery. However, the 10% needs to count. Setting up a meeting with a prospect or client and sleep walking into it is just asking for trouble. The meeting is where opinions about you, your company, your solutions and the value you offer are formed. It is where the foundations for the decision to work with you or not are laid. The more successfully you manage the meetings, the deeper the foundations.

Set out specific objectives to be achieved from every meeting—no matter how short or long the encounter is likely to be. Always be in control of the meeting, in a gentle but firm manner through the power of questions and the sharing of ideas. State your intentions clearly at the outset and summarise actions at the close. Smile more, use the person's name(s) more, exude warm confidence and always prepare for every eventuality.

Like Tom Cruise's character in the 1996 film *Jerry Maguire*, where Jerry was the master of the living room, be the master of the client meeting and the customer's buying cycle will work in your favour.

> Remember: Success is where preparation and opportunity meet.

Insight 104

The Matrix

You are in a typical sales meeting. The person across from you has challenges they may need to overcome. You, your product and your company may be the very thing they need to solve their problems. Your objective? To understand their challenges, discuss how you can help them achieve their goals and get them interested in doing business with you. So far so good, however, the thing about meetings is they can grow arms and legs and lead the party down unintended and sometimes needless paths that can produce little fruit within the small timeframe you have with the prospects, people that you have spent a lifetime trying to get in front of. So the obvious thing to do is to control the meeting—easier said than done, right? Maybe you should let something else take control. Your notes!

Yes your notes. Rainmakers know that taking notes the right way during meetings can help navigate the typical pitfalls and help them stay on track at all times, so they leave the meeting with both parties clear and happy with the outcome. Rainmakers recognise that there are typically four areas of information that need to be gathered from a meeting, particularly a discovery meeting. First is the background stuff, the information that will start you off in understanding the current scenario. Secondly, the problems, challenges and concerns the prospect or customer has. Thirdly, the right solutions that make sense to the prospect's specific situation.

Finally, the actions and next steps to move forward. By forming a "note matrix", you will be able to focus on what's important over what's not, giving you an evolving picture during the meeting and a clear snapshot after the meeting.

The Note Matrix

Background Information	
Problems, Challenges & Concerns	Solutions from Rainmaker Benefits
Action Points & Next Steps	

Remember: Customer face-time is crucial. Chance is not enough. Develop the note matrix.

Insight 105

It's all in the Nit-Picking

To be successful, there are many skills you as a sales professional need to develop in your career: prospecting, questioning, presenting, building rapport, time management, researching, closing, to name but a few. There is one skill though that helps add directly to your bottom line more than many others. What is this little-practised skill? It's the ability to *qualify*.

Warning: If you don't continually qualify your prospect's true intentions at every stage of the sales process as well as align those intentions up with yours, you will struggle to be truly effective and hitting targets will be more down to luck than skill. What are the odds on just pure luck?

If you are making an appointment, question yourself and the client about what the both of you would really want of the meeting.

If you are about to make a presentation, qualify the real reason for the presentation, who your audience will be and why they will be there.

If you are in a meeting, qualify who your prospect is and whether she is the M.A.N. (the person or persons with the Money, Authority and Need).

Qualify Everything! Get to the real heart of the matter always. That way, you will not waste time going to needless appointments, dealing with timewasters, closing prematurely or going to the wrong person and selling the wrong solution. All this timewasting will only make you less productive.

Remember:
If you are not
qualifying,
your
competitor is.

Insight 106

Two Little Letters

We have all heard of open questions and closed questions. You may have even been told that you use open questions to *open* your prospects up and closed questions to...well...*close* your prospects down. So we use open words like Who? What? Where? When? How? and closed ones like Can? Do? Is? So? Should? Would? Could? etc.

That's all well and good, and understanding the power of positioning these words at the right point in the conversation is certainly important. However, there is a word that is a really powerful pre-closer. This word works every time.

The word is "*if*". It's the pretext to the conditional close that can be used to close deals outright, or at the very least uncover new concerns during the customer's buying cycle that you can then address.

Here are some examples:

- "If I can demonstrate that our service can solve all the challenges you have stated in this meeting, would you be happy to raise an order?"

- "If I can show you a way to significantly reduce your operational costs, would you spare me 30 minutes of your time?"

- "If you are happy with the customer reference visit, what would be the next step?"

- "If by the end of this meeting you are happy with our solutions and all your concerns are met, would you be happy working with us?"
- "If we can meet those timescales, would you be in a position to proceed?"

The more powerful your questions, the more you uncover and the more effective your decisions will be from that point.

Remember: Harness the power of "if".

Insight 107

Your Company's Most Underrated Asset

We have all heard the popular sales adage: *people buy people.* By all accounts, this is true. Why? Because as humans, we are all wired to make a rational decision based on an emotional one. Put another way, we first make the decision based on how we feel about something, then we use rationale to justify this decision. This is why good salespeople understand the value in quickly building rapport and trust when forging relationships with prospects and customers. But...just like people, companies buy companies too.

Years ago I remember watching an old video of Steve Jobs presenting his company to an audience in 1980, four years after Apple Computer, Inc. started. Steve brought the story of his fledging firm to life, highlighting the vision, goals and opportunities to institute change within an ever-changing world for the benefit of everyone. It was an inspiring presentation. It also inspired me to want to deal with this computer company in some form. On some level, Steve's presentation had helped me tap into the *why* Apple are Apple and not so much into what they do and how they do it. Though the latter two areas are important, the foundation of partnership and trust forms when the customer begins to understand why your company exists.

I am forever perplexed when I witness a salesperson talk incessantly about how their company can provide this product or that service and how it can solve all the problems a prospect may have, but without providing an emotive reason to do business with the salesperson's company. In many cases, the salesperson doesn't even know what the company they work for actually stands for within their space.

Rainmakers spend time *getting* the firms they represent. They understand the company's vision, its goals and its unique way of wanting to make a difference. Rainmakers embody the *why* of the company and then tell the story in a way that the customer can understand and build trust on. Find out your why and tell your story.

> Remember: The most underrated asset your company has is the story of WHY. Use it to build trust.

Insight 108

Project-Managing the Sale

Football might be a simple game of two halves with the objective of scoring as many goals as possible, but "the special one", José Mourinho, is regarded as one of the best football managers on the planet because he knows that games are won or lost due to planning.

There are key stages in a typical sales process:

- Prospecting
- Qualifying
- Initial Contact
- Identify needs
- Cover the bases
- Propose Solution
- Evaluate Solution (including dealing with objections)
- Negotiate Terms
- Gain Commitment

Each stage has to be successfully completed in the client's eye if you want to ultimately achieve the deal. You enter each stage with a specific plan of action to achieve a specific objective.

At every stage of the process, take time out to evaluate where you are and what you need to do to be successful at that particular stage.

Write it all down. Be specific. Draw on the experience of others to determine the best ways to deal with a particular stage in the process. Conduct a "what if" analysis looking at various scenarios so that your plan of action takes *everything* into account. Put yourself in the prospect's shoes. Try and think the way they would. Document everything in your experience journal highlighted in the insight, *The Rainmaker's Guide to...* as these exercises can form your *experience pool*, which you can expand over time.

The message here is to be completely pragmatic when considering your next move, devoid of all emotion. Only think of commissions *after* your company have invoiced for the customer for the service. Your job before then is to always consider adding value to the client and closing the deal.

Remember: The less you let chance play a part the more chance will work in your favour.

Insight 109

They're Not Just for Science Projects...

The funnel is a useful physical tool if you are a mechanic, a chef or a biochemist. As a conceptual tool in sales for picturing where one is and where one ought to be relative to targets, the funnel is of paramount importance. It is a useful representation of your unique sales ratios (USR). It is an immediate indicator of how successful you are now and how successful you are *likely* to be.

Wikipedia defines a funnel as follows: *A funnel is a pipe with a wide, often conical mouth and a narrow stem. It is used to channel liquid or fine-grained substances into containers with a small opening. Without a funnel, spillage would occur.*

Let's analyse the essence of this statement through the eyes of the Rainmaker:

Your sales pipeline has a *wide* beginning and narrow *conclusion*. The two are *directly proportional*—that is, the fuller the *mouth* of the funnel is with qualified prospects, the better the *flow rate* of orders and customers appearing from the *stem* of the funnel.

Managing your process as well as developing and using the right skills at the right time, is equivalent to *channelling the liquid or fine-grained substances*. The more of a Rainmaker you are the more *pressure* you can create, thereby increasing the *flow rate*.

The aim of the game is to attract new business through gaining new customers thus more orders. This adds to your bottom line, profit and ultimately commissions. Using the funnel analogy, you have to find a way to capture as much business out there as you can and direct it into *containers with a small opening*. That opening is your firm's balance sheet and your own bank accounts.

Without a funnel, spillage would occur. If you don't guide your suspects to prospects to customers to loyal clients via your sales funnel, *spillage* will occur in the form of deals lost. There is only ONE place these deals go—your competitors. This is tantamount to transferring money from your firm to your competitor's bank account. Take away the time differential and that's exactly what it is. The more you manage your funnel, the less *spillage* will occur.

The Rainmaker is judged in the future on hitting targets but the Rainmaker is judged NOW on the state of her pipeline. The *conical mouth* has to be always brimming, the pressure in the funnel has to be high and constant, the flow rate of orders at the *stem* has to be consistent. Check your funnel's mouth is big enough. Check that you are working the pipeline with the pressure of your skillset and determination and make sure your flow rate is enough to hit and surpass your target. This is the Rainmaker's job. This is YOUR job. Develop the *Funnel Attitude* that permeates everything you do.

Remember: If it's not a funnel it's a conical flask, through which it'll be impossible to achieve your target.

Insight 110

When is a Problem Really a Problem?

People and companies buy to solve problems. It can be a straightforward problem like a person buying a car to solve a transportation problem or it could be more abstract, like a person buying a sports car to solve a lifestyle problem. Either way, purchasing happens when problems need to be solved. *Need,* however, is the operative word here. Customers will only do something about the problem if their *need* is perceived to be great enough to overcome the buying inertia. Many companies recognise that they have problems but don't necessarily think their *problem is really a problem* enough to justify a change.

To find the source problem is the beginning of the Rainmaker's quest for value. The real power however comes when the Rainmaker helps the client uncover the *true significance* of the problem, which may have a compounding effect on the business. At that point, the first of the Newtonian laws comes into play and movement begins.

I went to see a prospect once through a referral. I had done my research and analysed different scenarios that may cause a company to decide to upgrade their current system. The prospect was a pleasant enough person. I asked him why they had not upgraded their system in 20 years, he said it hadn't given the company any problems in that time. I asked how the company had changed in all that time, he informed me that they used to be manufacturing-based but over the last five years, all manufacturing had moved to Asia and they were now completely online-based. I delved deeper and it transpired that *all* business processes, transactions and storage were all dependent on their existing system. I *then* asked him questions about business risk management and the operational costs of running the system and in both cases they were high. The system formed the biggest risk to the business and it constituted the highest operational business cost by far. These two issues were the implications of the problem of doing nothing, yet they were not under the prospect's radar. *He hadn't thought of it that way.* With a newfound compound problem, he was decisive on action: a new system.

Your job is to turn a manageable problem into a compounded one by asking deeper questions. Questions that reveal the true significance of that problem. It's like in Charles Dickens' *A Christmas Carol*, where Ebenezer Scrooge is shown a *glimpse* of the implications of his actions, causing him to make different decisions afterward. Rainmakers are the projectors of the real problem.

> # Remember: Be the optician. Get the customer to see through a new lens.

Insight III

Helping to Solve the Puzzle

The 17th century French mathematician, physicist, inventor, writer and philosopher Blaise Pascal achieved many things in his lifetime. He invented the first mechanical calculator, which led to him being named after Niklaus Wirth's computer programming language (Pascal programming language), his contribution to mathematics (Pascal's theorem, Pascal's Triangle) is significant, he made great strides in physics (The Pascal—the SI unit of pressure). Pascal also however said something that enables Rainmakers to achieve so much more with prospects and customers than the average salesperson: *"People are generally better persuaded by the reasons that they have themselves discovered than by those which have come into the mind of others"*.

Many sales writers, gurus, trainers and managers always love to use the phrase: *Telling is not selling.* Merely stating product and service advantages, benefits and solutions to prospects can create resistance. However, by asking pre-planned and carefully crafted questions in order to establish the customer's problems and the implications to those problems, a dynamic develops that allows the prospect or customer to *discover* the unique solutions you offer with your guidance. That is Rainmaking.

With ever-increasing competition becoming so fierce, sales professionals and their companies can ill afford not to strive for excellence and perfection in persuading customers to buy. If you do not strive for perfection, you leave a gap. A gap that will certainly be filled by the competition. When all is said and done, it will always boil down to the things you say when interfacing with the client, the way you say them and the subsequent decisions you make to influence and therefore close the deal.

Start today to think on how you relate to your prospects at meetings. Do you rush in to demonstrating how you can help. Alternatively treat meetings like discussion seminars, where you set the stage for solutions to become natural outcomes of *peer-to-peer* discussions. Choosing to develop the skills that help you to excel at this will allow you to establish relationships with clients that are born out of respect, mutual understanding and reliance.

> Remember: Rainmakers provide the tools for the customer to figure things out.

Insight 112

Myopia and Hypermetropia

There is not a lot I remember about calculus when I studied maths in school. I still possess an image of our bearded maths tutor wearing the same burgundy knitted sleeveless pullover he wore every day. He would say, "There are two types of solutions when solving differential equations: *General Solutions* of an nth-order equation are solutions containing n arbitrary variables, corresponding to n constants of integration and *Particular Solutions* which are derived from the general solution by setting the constants to particular values, often chosen to fulfil set initial conditions or boundary conditions—oh, and don't worry about global and singular solutions for now…" You can see why I do not remember much.

Rainmakers are successful largely because they have this uncanny ability to simultaneously process and communicate the general and the particular. It is a skill that once witnessed is subconsciously used to differentiate the average salesperson from the Rainmaker. Imagine discussing your requirements with a salesperson who constantly talks "bigger picture", asking vague sweeping questions and shying away from detail. You would begin to think that person did not know their stuff. Equally, imagine the same scenario, but the salesperson talks incessantly about the nuts and bolts of the products and solutions without an understanding of where all of this was coming from in the first place. You would almost feel you were judging the national "know your product" competition. Both instances add little or no value to prospects and customers.

Rainmakers understand the bird's eye map view of situations and yet appreciate the ant's view within the territory. Rainmakers use this skill to *guide* the prospect on a journey from an initial *general* outline of requirements to a clear *particular* understanding of solutions and action plans. Rainmakers use this skill to develop pragmatic solutions based on customer's unique state of affairs. Rainmakers use this skill to demonstrate *real benefit*. This skill is rare. Develop and possess this skill and seldom will you cross the path of another who also has the gift.

> # Remember: Seeing beyond the seen is the Rainmaker's highest differentiator.

Insight 113

The Question Book

Growing up, if I did something wrong, I would always talk and charm my way out of the situation. My mother would say, "You always seem to have an answer for everything".

In Ben Younger's 2000 film *Boiler Room,* a senior broker (Nicky Katt) is advising the main character (Giovanni Ribisi) about objection handling: "...I have this friend who runs this other firm. He gives out this book to all his trainees. *The Rebuttal Book.* Looks like a Filofax. Has those index tabs but they don't say A to B to G to H, they say things like 'Wife won't let me', 'I'm not in the market now', 'Call me back', 'Send me a prospectus'. Has a rebuttal for any excuse..."

The rebuttal book may work in transactional sales as an objection handling reminder tool, but in consultative solution selling, one should always know how to add value by working through the concerns with the client throughout the sales process. Rainmakers, however, should develop and use the *Question Book.*

Questions are the drivers of the sales process. Ask the right question in the right syntax and you can go so much further in the sale than your competitors can. The question arises: *How can you confidently know the right questions to pose when in theatre?* The answer is to always think of the questions beforehand, write them down in your question book and constantly review them, update them, study them and practise them. In doing so, the matrix of queries will become second nature and when in theatre, your mind will naturally know what question to select and when.

You may be asking yourself *how do I develop these questions?* Here are some question areas to build your question book on:

- What would typically be your current situation?
- What problems would you be experiencing?
- What would the implications be to those problems?
- If not solved, how big or damaging can these problems get?
- What are the various things I can do to solve these issues?
- Can you tell me more?

Through the answers to these queries, you can ascertain typical questions you can further ask the client.

Always find and add new innovative, intelligent questions to ask, deeper questions that bring out even more information than planned, questions that really make the prospect think hard. Having and using the question book will end up being invaluable to you.

> Remember: Tools leverage. The secret weapon gives the edge. Use the question book as both a tool and a secret weapon.

Insight 114

Locomotion

You hear the term *business drivers* a lot these days. In fact, sales and businesspeople use it a lot in conversation, many a time completely out of context as it sounds like just another cool business phrase to have in one's head.

In reality, however, understanding the true concept of business drivers and using it as a qualification tool and a way to understand your prospects and clients can help you, the Rainmaker, increase your deal-closing hit rate.

So what are business drivers anyway? One definition is: Business drivers are *people, knowledge and conditions (such as market forces) that initiate and support activities for which the business was designed.* One way to look at it is that they are the catalysts that enable businesses to achieve their strategic and functional goals. These catalysts can be:

- A new product or service offering

- Pressures from direct and indirect competition

- The ever-changing demands and needs of their customer base

- Price, base cost and margin pressures

- Sales and market share pressures

- Growth—organic, through acquisition, or both

- The never-ending search for new revenue streams

- Share price performance

In any deal, it will be one or more business drivers such as the examples listed above that provide the fuel to run the sales process engine. The Rainmaker's job is to quickly identify the fundamental catalysts driving the prospect's business needs as well as effectively and elegantly demonstrate how, by your prospect working with YOU and your company; a successful outcome can be created from the drivers.

Try to imagine beforehand, through research, what the main business drivers are for your prospect. Have the answers in your head (or written down) before you meet and qualify. Start your questions from the business angle around goals and drivers, before naturally zooming in to more technical matters so that you leave with a good grasp of the wider business fundamentals as well as how the finer technical details bridge the catalyst gap.

> ## Remember: Use the knowledge of your customers' business drivers to drive your business forward.

Insight 115

...Enough to Make One Cry

Rainmakers see the process of a sales call—be it on the phone all face to face—as an opportunity to "peel the onion". As you know, one peels an onion one layer at a time. This is the only way to get to the real heart of the matter. Below is an illustration of this:

Prospect: Please send through a proposal…

Rainmaker: I would certainly love to. May I ask, what would be the most important issue you would like for the proposal to address?

Prospect: Well outside of price, system availability is critical to us.

Rainmaker: System availability? How would you define that internally?

Prospect: You see, our customers demand access to our systems 24/7/365 and it cannot go down…ever!

Rainmaker: I see, and what if the system did go down?

Prospect: As we are regulated by the state regulators, we would be fined at least $100K *per day.*

Rainmaker: ...and at the most?

Prospect: Well the state regulators have been known to fine a firm $2M a day.

Rainmaker: As much as that? Let's assume it got to that stage—what would be the impact on the way you do business?

Prospect: It will be disastrous for us: we would lose customers, then market share and our shareholders would not be happy, plus in this day and age we might never recover. That's why our CEO has made this her top priority.

Rainmaker: So if our solution ensured a fully resilient, highly available solution within the budget you stipulated, would you work with us?

Prospect: Yes.

Rainmaker: Let's talk about your budget...

The above example demonstrates the action of layering questions on top of each other, sticking to the same vein until you arrive at its natural conclusion.

Barristers do this all the time. When examining a witness they find an *onion* and they begin peeling away until they get to the real issue, before moving on to the next onion.

Rainmakers use this method of questioning because they know that two things will ensure their success over and above their competitors:

- **Information.** Knowledge is power, so getting ALL the information required will put you in good stead.

- **Decisions.** The actions you take based on the information obtained are critical to winning the order and thus the lifetime value of the client.

Like doctors, consultants and lawyers, you are there to ascertain the facts and act upon them.

Practise layering your questions always. Become good at it so that you end up performing this instinctively. Before every call, decide what key details you intend to obtain and stick to your plan.

> Remember: Getting to the heart of the matter with the prospect is your lift to the top. That's where the deals are closed.

Insight 116

Michelangelo di Lodovico Buonarroti Simoni

A definition of gap analysis in Wikipedia's is: *In business and economics, gap analysis is a tool that helps a company to compare its **actual performance** with its **potential performance**. At its core are two questions: "Where are we?" and "Where do we want to be?"*

A gap analysis (along with SWOT, PEST, five forces, the Boston Matrix, and other strategic analysis methodologies) is an important tool used to evaluate strategic intent—it adds value to decision-making. YOU as a Rainmaker should also use gap analysis as a selling tool to help prospects evaluate their requirements.

The key element of this tool is *questions*. Your questioning technique (the questions you ask, the way they are structured and layered) is critical in helping the customer establish a firm gap between where they are and where they should be. Going through this process in a structured and thorough manner is what adds value to the customer and sets you apart from your competitors.

Your questions should be based around key strategic business areas. Think about how to structure and layer your questions. Your aim in using these questions is to make the customer see just how wide the gap is, reinforcing the need to narrow the gap and its urgency by solving this problem through using your company and your solutions. The skill of using this tool is an integral part of your Rainmaking armoury.

The ceiling of the Sistine Chapel at the Vatican is awe-inspiring.

The detail and splendour of the paintings displaying Michelangelo's depiction of biblical concepts is truly spectacular. But that's just it, Michelangelo was an artist, who paints pictures of concepts that you can make sense of. His works help you decipher what could or should be relative to what is. That's what Rainmakers also do, the use GAP analysis to illustrate the chasm between what is and what could or should be, then they help you cross that chasm, bridge the gap if you will. That's the Rainmaker's job. That's your job.

Remember: You are the artist, the starker your painting of the gap is, the more motivated your client will be to bridge it.

Insight 117

Outlived Uselessness

The author of *The Seven Habits of Highly Effective People*, Stephen Covey, once said, "We simply assume that the way we see things is the way they really are or the way they should be. And our attitudes and behaviours grow out of these assumptions".

As human beings, we think our individual view of the world is the map, whilst in reality, it is simply our take on the territory we see. After all, in the Middle Ages everyone thought the world was actually flat.

Now making simple assumptions is acceptable in the normal interacting of people, but this is not something you should allow to lurk within the sales arena. This is a definite no-no! In fact, the evil habit of making assumptions is a real deal-breaker and target-killer.

I remember the courtroom drama movie I watched many years ago, *Philadelphia*. Denzel Washington's character, Joe Miller, always cross-examined the witness by stating: "explain this to me like I'm a four-year-old". My advice is that this is the attitude a Rainmaker should have. Act like a child when obtaining information, and assume nothing. Leave your ego at the door and ask questions with a completely *blank* mind.

Layer your questions on top of each other—i.e. question the answer to the question. This will give you a deeper understanding of the issues and it also gives you access to the minute details that can be the key to winning the deal.

Remember: The least questioned assumptions are often the most questionable.

Insight 118

Attention Seeker

Understanding your customers' needs requires two things from you. Your ability to ask the right questions and your ability to listen…really listen!

Most people take listening for granted. Do you ever feel, when your customer is talking, that your mind is "rehearsing" what you're about to say next? If the answer is yes, then what you are doing is called "passive" listening—that is to say, you are "hearing" what is being said but you are at the same time missing the "essence" of what is being said, the signals, the body language, the nuances—you are listening in black and white!

Really listening, really getting into the zone of absorbing the whole colour picture that the customer is communicating is called "active listening". It is not a talent; it's a skill that can only be learned through practice. The beauty is that you can practise active listening with anyone you care to listen to.

When you are in dialogue, empty your mind and concentrate on what the other person is trying to convey to you. Don't rush in to respond. In order to be understood, you must first seek to understand. Develop the skill of asking the right questions and listening actively, and the rest of the sales process becomes a lot easier.

Remember:
You have
TWO ears
and ONE
mouth. Stick
to that ratio.

Insight 119

In Communicado

Peter F. Drucker, one of the most revered management gurus of our time, once said: "The most important thing in communication is to hear what isn't being said".

Our only real tool as a *Rainmaker* is our communication skills, i.e. the ability to understand, process and convey information in a way that adds value and produces results. That's it! Everything else just supports that. Communicate well and you will surpass your competition every time. Yes, there are a myriad of skills you have to develop and master to be exceptional at the selling game but top of the list will always be communication.

Author of *SPIN Selling*, Neil Rackham, once stated that selling is about adding value, not communicating value. Although this is true, I believe you still can only add value *through communication* in all its forms: What you say, how you say it, what you do not say, how you do not say it, when you say or not say it, what you question, when you question, how you question, the answers you hear, your response to those answers, the way in which you respond, all non-verbal communication, how you communicate to yourself etc…

Also bear in mind that communication also refers to the written form as well: emails, quotations, proposals, tender responses and other business-related correspondence.

Think about how you are communicating with yourself and

others, what message you are giving out, how you are engaging and what your desired endgame would be.

> # Remember: Communication is a life skill that truly gives you life.

Insight 120

The Vernacular of Non-Language

In the 1960s, Albert Mehrabian, a Professor Emeritus of Psychology at UCLA, conducted a study of human communications. This study, now famously known as the *Mehrabian Communications Study*, concluded that when we communicate, we emotionally interpret only 7% of the meaning, or essence, of what is being said as verbal (i.e. the actual words), while 38% is the vocal (that is the tone, pitch and inflection of the voice) and 55% the body language and facial expressions.

Though the accuracy of this research has long been contested, what it does say to me is that the non-verbal "stuff" one does when communicating with another is of critical importance to how the recipient takes in what is being said and how they ultimately respond.

As a Rainmaker, you need to be in tune with how you communicate with your clients. You need to be aware how you come across in meetings, over the phone or even in a coffee shop!

Ask yourself questions like:

- How do I come across?

- How do I sound?

- What image am I trying to convey to my prospects?

- How do I make my first-time prospects feel at ease, and how do I get them to open up to me?

Be honest with yourself and improve your communication skills constantly...never stop.

Remember:
If your prospect forms the wrong opinion of you, chances are you will never know.

Insight 121

The Clarity of Certainty

Have you ever sat in traffic on a slight incline, all's well with the world and then suddenly the driver in the car behind you frantically starts thumping the horn? You immediately and instinctively apply the brakes, though at this stage you don't know why. Then it hits you, your car was actually rolling backwards without you actually realising it!

Sometimes when working on a particular deal or penetrating a certain key account, things may be standing still or moving backwards and you may not realise it, or worse, you may still be content that everything is great and you've reserved a particular Rolex watch to be bought with the commissions from that deal.

Rainmakers take nothing for granted at any stage of the buying cycle. They develop an inbuilt tachymeter and compass in the brain that constantly measures and records the speed and direction a sale or an account is going in. Rainmakers are therefore constantly readjusting their strategy and tactics based on what is happening within or outside of their sphere of influence. It is an on-going game of chess, made more complex because you are playing two games simultaneously: one with the account and one with competitors working on the same account.

When observing the Formula One Grand Prix, you can see that on average, it's the team that proactively reacts to the main challenges and the changing conditions that gets results. Changing parameters such as weather, tyre conditions, airflow, temperature, fuel consumption, engine management, other competitors and crashes are constantly being monitored. If the strategy and tactics of dealing with these conditions come together beautifully, chances are the (good) driver will get to stand on the podium.

Never stop asking yourself questions like:

- Is this deal moving in the right direction at the right pace?

- Am I clear as to what stage of the sale I find myself in?

- Who else in the account do I need to be influencing?

- Do I have the right insider and have I prepped that person?

- Do I understand the underlying drivers within the account that can potentially change things?

- Am I clear on who my competitors are in the account and on their respective capabilities?

- Is my strategy at this point the most effective one? What are my options?

You may well have more questions you could ask yourself. The purpose of this critical exercise is *account clarity*. Without that, you are taking off, flying and landing all on autopilot, which will never have a successful outcome and you may have to wait a little longer for that Rolex watch.

Remember: Clarity Begets Certainty. Be Clear. Be Certain.

Insight 122

The Anatomy of a Buying Conversation

There is a concept called *task-unrelated thinking*. This is where one mentally shuts down during a conversation and starts thinking about other things. This normally happens when a customer is not interested in what you are saying.

Sadly, this occurs all too often when the salesperson thinks they know what the prospect wants to hear but this is actually not the case and worse still, the prospect may even not steer you and simply say nothing. It's tragic when a prospect is staring at the salesperson and thinking: "*I can't believe he is selling to me when all I want is for him to help me solve my problem!*"

To avoid this scenario, you must set the *customer's conversation expectation*.

Each time you have a discussion with your customer, be it in a meeting or on the phone; ask them questions like:

- What are your expectations of this conversation?

- What information can I provide?

- What is the one area most critical to you right now?

Never assume you know what the customer wants. *Qualify Always.*

Remember:
Setting the
customer's
expectation
demonstrates
respect for the
customer and thus
for yourself.

Insight 123

No One is Fluent in Idiot

I visited my doctor's surgery the other day. When I arrived, I was told my regular doctor was away and a different doctor would see me instead. I obliged. On meeting me, the doctor proceeded to ask me a number of questions to which I responded. He then replied, spewing medical jargon with maybes and if-buts which all sounded like idiot speak to me. This continued for a few minutes before I had to stop him in frustration. "You really need to speak to me in plain English," I said, trying my best not to let my annoyance come through in my voice.

This scene is played out all over the world, particularly when "experts" are trying to convey information. In order to come across as having equal stature with others, they come out with technical terms, business "slang" and awful acronyms that seem to get longer and more meaningless by the day. As salespeople, we are crammed full of technical information and solutions that prospects and customers can benefit from. However, when communicating, one must convey information not only plainly but conversationally.

Communicating is about conversations. You ask, they respond; they ask, you respond; you both discuss, form conclusions and agree together. That's a conversation. That's Rainmaking. If Rainmakers have to use technical terms, they should be the prospect's terms of reference, not the salesperson's.

Rainmakers use practical examples, customer success stories and analogies to convey potentially complex concepts. William Penn, the famous real estate entrepreneur, Quaker and the founder of the Province of Pennsylvania once stated, "Speak properly, and in as few words as you can, but always plainly; for the end of speech is not ostentation, but to be understood".

Plain and clear speaking should be your hallmark in any conversation.

> # Remember:
> # You are
> # responsible for
> # what is said
> # AND for what
> # is understood.

Insight 124

Shut Up!

Salespeople are known to be great talkers. It's almost as if they are compelled to talk. We also know that selling is not talking, that the focus should be on asking the *right* questions, *actively* listening to the responses to those questions, communicating innovative solutions by discussing ideas and concepts and then ensuring the delivery of the tangible benefits that you propose.

Communication however is not necessarily just about words. There is an old African proverb that says, *"Silence is also speech"*. Deliberately pausing in a conversation says many things to the people you are talking to. Rainmakers know that they will need to be adept at the art of using silence to achieve certain outcomes.

Here are three ways one could use silent pauses in conversations:

1. When you ask a probing question, pause. Stay silent for as long as it takes for the prospect to have fully responded to you. This shows that you respect the person enough to give them time and space to consider your question and it gives you the opportunity to become more attentive to the non-verbal signals they may be displaying, which you can then react to.

2. If you feel an answer to your question is incomplete, you can simply nod and smile and *wait silently.* If there is more to come, the prospect may be compelled to volunteer more information.

3. When asking for commitment, be it to progress to the next stage or to ask for the order, ask and *pause.* Say nothing. Zip up. Wait for the prospect to respond. Eventually the prospect will either come up with an objection or agree to your proposal.

Using silence can be daunting at first, as it can seem natural to break your own silence if more than two seconds of non-verbal communication have taken place. Training yourself to understand and use silence to your advantage can end up being another tool to help the sales process along, as well as ensuring you are seen as a true value-generating professional and not just another quick-talking peddler of goods and services.

> # Remember: If you are comfortable with silent pauses, your customer will end up being comfortable with you.

Insight 125

Socratica

In the early days of my selling career, I met up with my mentor, David, for breakfast one day. David was a tall, slender, well-groomed man in his late fifties, with piercing blue eyes and a face with very few wrinkles for his age. We chatted about the weather for a while and out of the blue he asked, "How does selling make a difference to the world?"

I stopped chewing part of my egg benedict and looked up, asking myself "why such a question so early in morning?" I thought about it for a couple of seconds and replied, "I think industry cannot exist without good salespeople".

David smiled wryly. "Isn't it the other way round? Doesn't industry first design solutions to world problems before the need to sell anything?

I paused to think about that one. "So are you saying that in actual fact it's the inverse: salespeople cannot exist without industry?" I said, feeling a debate brewing in the air.

"You could look at it that way, or you could say it has nothing to do with salespeople or industry but about selling,"

"I'm confused now".

"As a concept, it all starts with selling—everything. Someone has to sell the need to a problem before the design even begins in the first place. If you think of the sale as the foundational act which every other discipline is built on, then it's easier for you to see how selling has always made a difference to the world".

For several years I thought about this brief eye-opening conversation I had with David. More recently, however, what became even more eye opening to me was the *structure* of that conversation. The *way* David phrased his questions reminds me of the *Socratic method* of questioning.

The 400 BC Greek philosopher Socrates had an extremely effective way of opening up his *"question everything"* presupposition with fellow philosophers and students alike. His questions forced you *to critically evaluate* your current paradigm. These questions and subsequent statements can make you actively see new ways of thinking, new attitudes, and new paradigms. He famously stated, *"I cannot teach anybody anything; I can only make them think".*

This method of questioning, once mastered, turns conversations with prospects and clients into powerful enablers that can shake up their views of the "status quo" within their own organisations and consider the merit of new ways to incorporate the value you, the Rainmaker, can add by helping to solve their problems.

Think long and hard about how you get your customers to scrutinise the way they are doing things, the way they evaluate your competitors, the way they intend to solve their problems. Practise asking these questions. Design and practise wow statements that stop their thought processes dead in their tracks and make them focus on you. Think Socrates.

> Remember: It's thoughts and actions that change everything. Rainmakers strive to influence both!

Insight 126

The Most Powerful Killer Sales Question of all Time

There are questions and there are questions. I deem the *killer questions* as those that have a massive impact due to the importance of the answer given or the decisions made because of the question posed.

Rainmakers believe that the most powerful killer sales question is something like this:

"What would you feel is the best way to achieve this goal?"

There it is, in all its splendour and glory. Deceptively simple, isn't it? Killer questions normally are. The power to this question is two-fold, like two sides of the same sword. On one side, the question gets the prospect or customer to "design" a solution that fits them. Like a soon-to-be homeowner who discusses the details of the new build with an architect, this question forces you to take the place of the architect in this dynamic. However, this side of the sword cannot work without the other side, which is setting the prospect up to properly receive the question in the first place such as building rapport and trust, asking the right preluding questions about their issues and drawing out the implications of their problems before aiming and firing the killer question.

Once the prospect describes what the solution would look like, Rainmakers simply add meat to the bone until all parties are clear and committed.

This is my top killer question. If you don't agree, the question should be "what's yours?"

> Remember: The "Divas" of the sales conversation are the killer questions, all other forms of communication are there to support them. Develop and use your KSQs.

Insight 127

The Benefit System

If you ask the average salesperson this question, *"what is the difference between a feature, an advantage and a benefit?"* you will likely get an answer along the lines of:

"OK, I think a feature is fact or statement about a product or service such as 'this electric car is equipped with a 90kW-hr battery pack'. An advantage is essentially what the feature does. So, keeping with the electric car example…the 90kW-hr means you can go much faster for longer between charges. And finally, the benefit really demonstrates the true value of the advantage…therefore the cost of running the car is less due to less charging".

Now all this makes sense. But what if the customer has no regard for the battery size? What if the value is in the design of the car, or the socio-political statement the prospect wants to show in just having an electric car on his driveway? In reality, Rainmakers know that there is a subtle distinction between features and advantages and the benefits the customer values. What is that distinction? Yep, you guessed it. The distinction is *value*.

Rainmakers are acutely aware that every customer, department or organisation is different, with unique goals, needs, wants and value characteristics. When using FAB (features, advantages benefits) statements, salespeople reel off the features, advantages and benefits without always considering what is important to that particular customer within that particular deal.

Rainmakers know their product features, advantages and benefits inside out and upside down. What they do however is keep that information in reserve and only access what is required for the prospect to gain the value needed. They start with powerful questioning that qualifies and clarifies the goals and needs. Then, and only then, do they align those needs with a FAB statement where a feature, advantage and benefit are wrapped into a value proposition centred around helping the prospect attain a desired outcome. When making FAB statements, Rainmakers use the ratio: 10% feature, 20% advantage and 70% benefit giving them 100% value. It's the direct-hitting benefits that close deals.

> # Remember: A synonym for the word "value" is "benefit". Customers only buy value.

Insight 128

New Wavelength Required

The Internet has changed everything. The way we communicate, the way we transact, the way we relate to the world, the way we learn. The Internet has also changed the way corporate customers buy.

There was a time customers relied on salespeople for technical and commercial information about "what's out there?" and "what should we be considering?". Sir Tim Berners-Lee changed all that with the advent of the World Wide Web. Today, users and decision-makers alike can research and find anything they need such as specifications, benchmarks, user experience case studies, or whatever else is necessary.

In reality, the only reason why users and buyers *think* they need salespeople is to beat them up on price with a selfie stick!

Buying companies need Rainmakers for another reason, however. They need Rainmakers to help them make sense of all this information. They need Rainmakers for *insight*.

Rainmakers have exposure. They have exposure to their existing clientele who also had to solve problems with the Rainmaker's solutions. They have exposure to different industries and possibly different regions. This exposure gives them a huge advantage over decision-makers whose only real exposure is within the confines of the companies, industries and regions they work in. Rainmakers turn all this exposure into insight. What is insight? It's an eclectic mix of knowledge, evidence, experience and a touch of innovation, which can be turned into practical ideas that will help companies in need. Decision-makers need education on new perspectives on reaching their goals. They need a collaborative experience with Rainmakers who are on an equal footing.

The question you need to ask yourself is, "Am I able to spend an hour with a prospect and have him end up saying *'I would have easily paid a consultant for that hour'*"?

Use the information, knowledge and experience you have access to, transform them into insights, and begin to add the value your prospects and clients crave.

> # Remember: Customers have more to lose than you do if they make a wrong decision. Help them make the right one.

Insight 129

The Customer's Customer Relationship Management

Sometimes it's important to stop and ponder on what's important to your client. Most of the time, prospects go through the buying process and seek value from Rainmakers for one reason: *Their own customers.*

Every business needs them. That's why businesses exists. The more companies think about adding value to their customers, the more the company thrives. It pays to train yourself to see your customer through the lens of *their* customers. It's worth remembering that what you sell and do is part of a *value chain* and that recognising where you fit in the set of links can help you understand what your prospect or client is looking for.

Your focus as a Rainmaker is to determine the prospect's "hot buttons" when asking questions, provide well thought-through and innovative solutions and then gain agreement to move forward. By appreciating the customer's own clients' needs, you add colour and clarity to this process.

Here are some ideas to consider:

- Research your prospect's core values. This can be via their website or if a listed company, their online annual report.

- Find out what their industry says about them through news

sites, always keep an eye out for new developments within the prospect.

- Who are their customers? How do they market and service those customers: B2B, B2C, distribution, etc.

- Look at ways your prospect's competitors are doing things that may be different.

- From the information you glean, try to imagine how what your company does can help them better serve the needs of their clientele and formulate questions around those thoughts.

- Create ways to illustrate propositions that demonstrate you are thinking about them as a business and not just running the "sales" mill.

If you get this right and your customer begins to understand and acknowledge what you are trying to do, you have a way of "locking in" the relationship, which can only increase your residual income.

> # Remember: The value you add goes far beyond your customer. It pays to know this.

Insight 130

Sales Cycology

Imagine all the deals where the decisions were not made in your favour. Your insider tells you truthfully that it was so close, that you *almost* won that deal. The old saying "there are no prizes for second best" is so pertinent and starkly evident in the selling game.

There are a myriad of reasons why one would win or lose a deal. A proportion of the reasons could be completely outside of the sales professional's control. However, many of the reasons are down to what you do proactively in the *sales cycle*.

I sometimes liken the sales cycle to Formula One motor racing. There is a certain mind-set you have to possess when you are racing at such speeds round the circuit. You have other skilled drivers all around you. Although there is a set way round the course, things change on a second-by-second basis. Yes, you have to rely on your team for support, but it is ultimately down to you and the machine. You have to adapt to changing conditions, communicate effectively with your support team and learn from experience within the race and from every race. At the same time, the circuit is the circuit, there is a tried and tested method of going around a particular track. Formula One drivers know this method implicitly and all they do is consistently aim to improve on what they already know.

Rainmakers and Formula One drivers are similar. Rainmakers know the methodology of dealing with the sales cycle. Whether it is at the first meeting where the prospect is unsure as to what their solution should be, or in a tender situation, or falling into a process that is already at an advanced stage. Rainmakers are able to read conditions and adapt accordingly. Rainmakers are able to communicate effectively to prospects, colleagues, suppliers and other business associates alike. Most of all, Rainmakers orchestrate. They see all the *components* of the sales cycle and effectively *click* them all together to win the deal.

Always try to possess a bird's eye view of the sales cycle when you are *in* the sales cycle. Don't just operate from within the territory, use the map too.

> # Remember: Watch where you are going and how you will get there when Rainmaking.

Insight 131

⌐ A Circle in a Spiral Gets You Nowhere

Years ago, I received a call from a large multinational corporation asking for a direct quotation. Through my initial qualification I determined a clearer understanding of their requirements and sent through a quotation. I was full of anticipation, I felt that a deal like this would not come very often and I had just leapfrogged to the penultimate stage of the customer's buying cycle. Ultimately, it took two years and many meetings, designs, proposals and quotations to achieve the order all in the midst of a hyper-competitive environment. It was not so easy after all. I had made a costly disconnect which almost cost me the deal, but what had I disconnected?

Understanding the buying cycle is important. You need to be clear as to what stage of the customer's buying process you find yourself at in order to determine the strategies and tactics to use and the resources you must draw upon to be successful. However, the question arises: *does the customer work towards the same cycle as the salesperson?*

The answer is *of course not*. Rainmakers know that real and lasting sales success comes through determining the outcomes within the buying stages that the customer controls.

In its simplest form the buying cycle can be just three stages: *awareness, consideration and decision.*

I hate shopping for clothes. However, I love window-shopping for them. If I have some time, I would wander into a department store and browse the suits section with no real intent to buy. If I see something interesting, I would make a mental note of it and move on. If a store salesperson approaches me, I would be polite and interested but the chances of me buying at that point would be remote as I would be in the awareness stage. Contrast this to a change in circumstance, say a wedding coming up that weekend and I now *needed* the suit: I would march straight into the store with a focus on the decision to buy as I would now in the decision stage.

I know this is a very simple example but the stages are not that different within a complex business-to-business selling environment. What is interesting is that I have known salespeople who have attempted to push through the entire sales cycle within the awareness stage of the customer's buying cycle and wondered why the order didn't arrive.

Rainmakers align the sales and buying cycles to achieve success. They influence the customer within a stage and in order to transition to the next stage, knowing all the time that the customer and their environment determines how the cycle develops.

Think like a Rainmaker, who thinks like the customer. Think about the customer's goals, needs, timescales, the reasons behind their motivations and most importantly, their stages in the cycle. Then just ask...

> # Remember: How they buy determines how you sell.

Insight 132

The Mysterious life of the Proposal

The proposal is the most important document a salesperson can produce within the sales process. This document has to be all things to all people in the prospective account. It has to sell you to all sorts of individuals in your absence and it has to answer a myriad of questions posed by people in the account when you're not there. Knowing how and when to develop and distribute such a document is a skill critical to sales success.

Best-selling fiction writers go through life developing ideas, stories and characters for their work. They research by going to locations, meeting people, asking questions, generally engaging in conversation. They watch people and processes, they see how people live, interact and deal with situations. They try to put themselves in those situations. They are constantly imagining the story and making notes months and sometimes years before they write the book. In fact, the book is simply the culmination of all their research and ideas written in a structured form.

Rainmakers do the same. They start the proposal development from the very first encounter with the very first contact within the prospective account. Rainmakers know that one individual without any outside influence whatsoever very rarely decides on deals. Normally, particularly with complex enterprise sales, interested parties have to OK the deal before the M.A.N. (the person/s with the money, authority and need) signs it off (see *Baseball*). These parties could be the people using the solution, the people agreeing the funds, the people implementing the solution etc.

These different groups speak different languages and need to make sure their point of view is satisfied before they individually give their green light. Therefore, the proposal needs to be like a kaleidoscope reflecting the various views of the players. Rainmakers endeavour to speak to all parties involved *before* authoring the proposal. Rainmakers find out each contact's particular needs and how the Rainmaker's solution can meet those needs.

Finally, it's important to know that the most vital section in the proposal is the executive or management summary at the beginning of the document. That part is exclusively for the M.A.N. Apart from the price at the end of the proposal, real decision makers read nothing else within the proposal. The rest of the document is there to *justify* whatever the summary states, which will need to be endorsed by the other players. Rainmakers write the summary last and spend more time on these few lines than possibly the rest of the document as it has to convey a powerful message in a simple yet elegant way and that is no easy feat.

Don't just re-harsh proposals, or write them too early in the process. Do what Rainmakers do and get your story and facts straight first.

> Remember: Equip the proposal with everything it needs to thrive independently within the prospective account.

Insight 133

What They See is What They Get

Selling in the pharmaceutical industry can be challenging. One of the main problems is that pharmaceutical sales professionals with limited or no medical training have to sell medicines to *clinicians*. The focus for doctors therefore is the *reality* of the medicine, not the *marketing message*. Where are the double-blind studies data? What are the findings from the drug trials (human or otherwise)? What are the potential proven side effects? The questions keep rolling. To counteract this and to really add value to their clients (the doctors), the sales methodology adopted by these Rainmakers can be called *evidence based selling*.

One of the quickest ways to innovate and thus grow in any industry is to learn how other industries achieve success. Evidence-based selling is something we can all learn. The focus here is simple: *"demonstrating the empirical and factual reality of the value offered rather than just communicating the marketing message"*.

Customers are only customers because they have a goal to achieve or a set of challenges that need resolving. Consistently spinning the company and product/service spiel can nowadays seem almost rude. Rainmakers take great pains to go through the process of understanding the prospect's issues from a 360-degree standpoint, presenting a set of practical and demonstrable solutions backed up with facts, figures, examples, case studies, client references and workshops. Rainmakers never say things that cannot be easily and thoroughly verified.

Learn to prepare all the evidence for your pitch beforehand. This includes all the unexpected details. This will go a long way to prove your sincerity and integrity.

Evidence, however, works both ways. As one qualifies throughout the sales process, decisions should be made purely based on the evidence the prospect demonstrates. Be in a position to qualify your prospects consistently based on real facts. This will also aid you in providing yourself and management with real evidence of where you are with a particular deal, and more importantly, *why*.

Think like a lawyer. Work with facts and facts alone and you will gain the trust of all those around you.

> # Remember: Selling is all mirrors and no smoke.

Insight 134

The Deal in a Parallel Universe

What is the difference between the *price* of what you sell and the *cost* of what you sell to customer? The price can be seen as the monetary value placed on what you sell. The cost to the customer however is so much more.

Imagine the internal politics, egos and fears the decision-maker has to contend with within her organisation on a daily basis. Buying decisions, regardless of how complex and systematic they may appear, are personal decisions. Those decisions are based on what I like to call the *perceived consequential costs (PCC)* of that choice.

The cost to the customer can be viewed in both tangible and intangible terms. The tangible is based on the accepted monetary value of what they intend to purchase. The intangible is based on the ultimate cost, positive or negative, to them and their company if they choose you. It's the ultimate risk they have to weigh up. After all, IBM grew on the infamous slogan: "No one ever got fired for buying IBM!"

Rainmakers *always* think in *PCC* terms when going through the sales process with the prospect. The Rainmaker always tries to search for the perceived consequential costs of doing business with them. By talking to users, influencers and insiders, the Rainmaker can uncover these perceived consequential costs and work with the decision-makers to clarify and reassure.

In the James Cameron's 1984 movie *The Terminator*, Michael Biehn's character, Kyle Reese, was sent from the post-apocalyptic future to protect Sarah Connor (Linda Hamilton) from the Terminator (Arnold Schwarzenegger). Throughout the movie, the decisions and actions of all the characters were based on their perceived consequences in the parallel future world.

Your job is to exist in two parallel worlds during every sales cycle. The first is the real world in which you are in the process of selling the solution. The other is the parallel world where you can see the bought solution being implemented and the potential issues and problems that can arise *in that particular company.* By understanding the prospective account more, you can visualise the parallel future world and address those issues *now* with the decision-maker.

Always ask yourself: *"If I were to deal with **my** company and buy **my** solution, what risks would I be taking, what fears would I have, what would concern me?"* Put yourself in their shoes and jot your answers down. From your answers, formulate deeper questions that can draw out these concerns so that you can address them.

> Remember: The customer forever knowing they made the right choice of company and solution is the true value of the Rainmaker.

Insight 135

Please, Sir, I Want Some More!

In these difficult economic times with increased competition, it may appear an appropriate tactic is to drop your prices to win the business. This may be the desire of the commission-hungry salesperson, but razor-thin margins can be catastrophic for your business. The Rainmaker knows this.

Here is a shocker for you: In this uncertain business climate, customers would rather pay *more* than less! That's right, more. Why? You might ask. The reason is encapsulated in one word, *risk*. Making buying decisions, particularly for high capital, business-critical solutions is risky business for the decision-maker and ultimately the company. When times are good, the wrong decision could mean egg on one's face or in the worst case, the decision-maker's job. However, in times like these, with whole industries transforming and businesses going under daily, the wrong decision can cost the company significant market share, redundancies or even bankruptcy.

Therefore, in these harsh economic times, companies will happily pay a premium to mitigate any risk to their business. So, what does that mean? It means *You are in the insurance business.* Your job is to use every resource at your disposal to gain the trust of the client, to give customers compelling reasons to place their faith in you as a Rainmaker.

Value creation starts from the very moment the sales cycle

begins. From day one, demonstrate you're in the business of solving problems through trust. Constantly prove to your customers that you are a safe pair of hands through your technical expertise, your professional services skills, but mostly show value through your actions.

> # Remember: Don't just drop your pants, instead, offer them to the cliff-hanging prospect and pull him back up to the summit and he will reward you.

Insight 136

The Big Reveal

Revealing the price of a product or service is a fundamental part of the sales process. For a transaction to take place the seller has to show the price and the buyer has to agree to it. Rainmakers appreciate one simple principle here:

The timing of when the price is disclosed is more important to the success of the deal than the price itself.

The only real currency a salesperson has when interacting with a buyer is the price of the final offering. The buyer wants it and the salesperson possesses it.

Rainmakers know that prospects don't buy products or services; they buy the value created. This value can either help them solve problems or it can be used as a building block to create more value to pass on to *their customers*. The more value they perceive will be gained, the less of an issue pricing will ever be. Therefore the key is not the price point, but that you communicate the price *after and only after* you have unravelled the customer's most pressing needs, demonstrating how you, with your company, can add value to meet those needs *and* have obtained agreement that the uncovered *need–value equation* is indeed correct.

The Rainmaker wears many hats, one of which is that of a teacher. She sometimes has to *educate* the prospect on the full implications of their requirements and the real essence of the value the Rainmaker creates. To get *that* wrong renders the perceived value redundant and puts the spotlight on the price, which is where margins get squeezed or, worse still, the prospect gains an impression that your company is "all price and no value", over that of a competitor who can add value—bad news!

Rainmakers must be master detectives to get to the heart of the matter, they must be master communicators to illustrate value and they must be master value creators themselves. Only then will price never be an issue.

> # Remember:
> # Pertinent Probing
> # Plus Powerful
> # Propositions
> # Precedes Price.

Insight 137

What's the Value of a Life?

Adverts are always interesting, particularly print ads with witty one-liners that try to capture the essence of the product, service or experience the vendor is selling. An old (pre-Oracle) PeopleSoft advert hit the nail on the head of one of the core philosophies of Rainmakers. The caption stated, *"Customers are an investment. Maximize your return"*.

Several studies show that it costs several times more to acquire a new customer than to keep an existing one. The key to growth in any enterprise is to keep customers spending for as long as possible. Marketers give this concept various tags such as the lifetime value and the customer net present value. Rainmakers however, realise that when searching for new business, one must bear in mind the *future net worth* of the prospect. This should form a significant part of the qualification process. By determining early whether the prospect wants a value-added long-term relationship will aid you in deciding the amount of time, resources and effort you *invest* in winning the account and what happens thereafter.

There are a number of formulae for calculating the potential lifetime value of a customer. To me, the simple way is to take the top five loyal customers in your company, add up the total revenue and profit margin over the last five years adjust for inflation, then form an average and hey presto, you have a rough figure to get started with. Have that figure in mind when searching for your next lifetime customer.

By nurturing and developing *your few clients* through adding value, you could be creating the next top five customers for the company, enough to hit targets consistently year on year.

> # Remember: The real potential value of the customer is unlocked long after the first sale has been made.

Insight 138

Rules of Engagement

Donald Trump may have been a divisive political figure during the 2016 US Republican Party presidential primaries but watching Trump *trump* 16 other Republican candidates was, if anything, entertaining and thought-provoking. Trump used several strategies and tactics to become the Republican nominee. Many of them appeared unpleasant but one strategy stuck out for me that Rainmakers use all the time.

From day one, Trump was considered an "outsider", someone who was not a politician and therefore would be ineffective. Firstly, Trump turned this into a unique selling point (USP). Secondly, Trump somehow got the media and the public to define the rules of engagement of the 2016 Republican Party primaries to be about political insiders versus outsiders. Trump wasn't the only outsider (neither Ben Carson and Carly Fiorina were politicians) but he became the outsider to beat. Trump was able to make his USP *become* the focus of the 2016 Republican Party primaries.

Regardless of one's views on Trump's sensibilities and politics, getting your USPs to define the basis of a deal puts you and your solution in the driver's seat. Rainmakers achieve this by being part of the buying process early and helping to set the stage based on their solutions and the tangible benefits the prospect will receive. When other competitors eventually enter the fray you become the one to beat. As at this point you and the prospect have both invested time, energy and resources in getting to the "right" desired outcome.

The question then arises: When is early? The answer is simple: *Whenever they don't think they have a problem!* Opening conversations, getting to know the prospect, developing the relationship and showing them a better way can happen at any time. There is no time like the present. Start today to identify, contact and develop relationships with prospects that you believe will benefit from your USPs even if they don't know it yet. Make you and your solution define the rules of engagement.

> # Remember:
> # Design the board
> # you play chess on.

Insight 139

Money Talks

Rainmakers do not sell a product or service but a solution to a need. Rainmakers sell clients the ability to keep their vital businesses running uninterrupted so that they can remain competitive and grow.

A powerful way to influencing the prospect is always thinking and demonstrating in return on investment terms. Companies no longer spend, they *invest,* and your job is to show how investing in you is a wise move, for the company *and* the individuals making the investment.

When dealing with customers, particularly of a senior level within the organisation, demonstrate how the total cost of ownership (upfront and running costs) of the final solution will make them better off than they are *now.* Do your research on all the variables such as typical business costs (staffing, equipment, buildings, utilities...whatever). Understand financial management principles, analysis and ratios. Ask questions beyond just your industry area to find out what the financial "hot buttons" are that you can use to develop a ROI model that is important to them.

Remember: The lowest-priced solution is not necessarily the lowest cost to the client and customers buy on cost, not price.

Insight 140

Espionage? Well, Sort of

Trying to work an account and win deals can be a tough job. Today's selling environment involves more decision-makers, more influencers and steering committees all within one single account! Let's not even begin to talk about getting around the various internal politics, the different egos and the varying motivations in the account. How does one navigate this maze of haze to arrive at the order? How do Rainmakers do it? It is simple. Rainmakers cheat. They have the *insider*.

Sales gurus use numerous other names for this individual. Neil Rackham dubs them *sponsors* whilst Miller and Heiman call them *coaches*. Regardless of the terminology, the insider's purpose remains the same. They are your eyes, ears, navigator, promoter, negotiator and advocate. Without them, you will be stumbling through the process in complete darkness.

Recruiting an insider begins at the very start of the sales process. They will show you what to do, and what or whom to avoid, and they will be speaking on your behalf when it matters. This person should know the prospective company inside out, have some influence and, most importantly, be on your side. Stay close to the insider, ask them the right questions and coach them on doing your selling for you when it counts. But be warned: don't get distracted and become confused with their status in the overall strategy. Insiders are rarely decision-makers. Only use them for what they were recruited for. Recognise you also have other *users, influencers and decision-makers*. Be sure to concentrate your attention and efforts accordingly.

Do what Rainmakers do: recruit, develop and use an insider, and the odds on winning will start to work in your favour.

> # Remember: Don't be left out in the cold, leaving the competition holding the hot cocoa by the fire with what would have been your client. Get an insider!

Insight 141

The Hunter and the Hunted

Around 10,000 years ago, something outstanding occurred. Humans discovered agriculture. Before that point, we all were hunter-gatherers. Out of this emerges Thom Hartmann's *hunter vs. farmer* evolutionary hypothesis.

The corporate sales community have known about and debated the hunter and the farmer analogy for many years. If you are a "hunter", you're meant go out and seek the business using your "opening and closing" skills to bring in the lucrative accounts. Once the account has been won, if you are a "farmer", your job will be to develop, maintain and protect the account over the long term. The presupposition here is that hunters and farmers have different personalities and skills sets that predestine them to their respective role.

Here is a question. If the farmer just needs to have the skills to maintain and protect the account, whom would he/she be protecting the account from? *Other hunters!* As you can see, there would potentially be a skills mismatch and probably an unfair fight on the farmer's hands. Gone are the days where to keep an account churning all you had to do was visit once in a while, do lunch, play the odd round of golf, hand over the Christmas hamper and simply take orders. With competition escalating on an almost monthly basis and coming from the most unlikely sources and with customers being less loyal, there is no room for just farming anymore.

Equally, the notion of the one-dimensional set of skills that would constitute a hunter is increasingly becoming counterproductive. It is folly to see the nature of the archetypical hunter as restless, impatient, myopic and commission hungry and the farmer as laid back, organised and relationship-building. These qualities may serve the salesperson in a smaller transactional sale but may only harbour resistance in the larger, more complex corporate selling environment where value is the only currency. With customers just wanting to trade in value, there is no room for just hunting anymore.

What one needs to be is neither the hunter nor the farmer *and* yet both the hunter and the farmer. Incorporating the best of both worlds creates the well-rounded and equipped professional to do the job in *all* situations. That job is to sell. That individual is the *Rainmaker*.

> # Remember:
> # Don't just hunt or farm. Make Rain.

Insight 142

Account = Cluster of Deals

US basketball coach, author and motivational speaker Kevin Cook famously said, "You are only as good as your last game, and our last game was pretty doggone good". In the game of selling, there is a similar proverbial adage, "You're only as good as your last sale". Rainmakers are acutely aware that their livelihoods and careers are constantly a heartbeat away from disaster through lack of sales. They know that salespeople who cherish past wins more than desire future sales will stagnate and ultimately flat line.

Curiously, customers can express the same sentiment. Note this: Just because you closed a deal with a particular customer doesn't mean the account is yours. Trying to keep the account happy after your deal ultimately means very little. It will always come back to the same denominator: *"You're only as good as your last deal with us".*

The one and only way to develop an account is to seek out more opportunities and close more deals in that account. As long as you are somewhere in the sales process at any one time in the account, however small, then you are developing the account. If not, your last deal with them, no matter how recent, guarantees nothing.

Remember:
The deal is not
the account
and the
account is not
the deal.

Insight 143

Read More Than Just Books...

Selling by committee is an important and very real facet of this game.

Imagine, if you will, you sat in front of a steering committee of a prospective customer you are selling to. What do the individuals round the table see when they look at you? They may see a sales professional pitching for the deal or they may see something else: *Your competitor's competition!*

People are people and people buy from people. There is always a strong chance that in a new business scenario, you are not that person. You might be sitting in front of them, but for whatever reason, your prospect may well have their loyalties elsewhere. Not recognising this fact may incapacitate you as a Rainmaker.

In Taylor Hackford's 1997 film *The Devil's Advocate*, Keanu Reeves' character, Kevin Lomax, possessed a skill that made him never lose a case: he could read the individuals on the jury panel and make decisions accordingly based on his continual assessment of the jury relative to the trial. This skill (apparently) brought him to the attention of Al Pacino's character, John Milton.

Rainmakers always assess their chances at *every* stage of the sales process and continually ask themselves questions like: How do I influence this particular individual? How does the prospect view my company and the value being offered? Where do I place my focus in order to progress and ultimately close this deal? How do

I convincingly demonstrate our value over the competition? Do I pull out now? Do I hold?

Due to globalisation, turbulent economic realities, increased competition and increasingly complex packaged solutions, buying cycles are becoming longer and more protracted. Therefore, the cost of sale is constantly going up. It is becoming increasingly costly to go through the sales process repeatedly and not get results. The ability for the sales professional to consistently assess and decide is more valuable now than ever before. Develop this ability and success will be your crown.

> # Remember: A Rainmaker without sound judgement is like a blindfolded Olympic athlete performing the 100m hurdles.

Insight 144

Margin Call

In March 2016 the horse *California Chrome*, ridden by Victor Espinoza and trained by Art Sherman, won the 21st renewal of the Dubai World Cup and received $6m. This was the largest prize in horse racing history. Now think of *Mubtaahij*, the horse that came second. The runner-up's prize money was a fraction of the winner's at $2m. However, the differences between the two horses, jockeys and trainers were infinitesimally small. The winner won by *the slimmest of margins*.

It's the same in our profession, but in our case, there are no prizes for coming second. The winner gets the order and will likely continue to receive orders from that client for years to come.

Forget how many miles you are moving in your career! Inches count! Every detail, every proposal, every meeting, every phone call and every dialogue with the customer—it all counts towards orders, towards achieving your targets.

Every day, aim to get a little bit better, smarter, sharper, technically aware, business savvy. Aim to be the Rainmaker in your industry and you will invariably win the deals by the slimmest of margins.

Remember:
Make peace
with the
small inches.

Insight 145

Intra Deal Competitive Analysis

We all analyse (or rather, we *should* analyse) our competition generally. A simple tool to achieve this is a SWOT analysis. Examining your strengths and weaknesses of the competition, evaluating where the opportunities lie and what threats to be aware of will help you make decisions around your strategy. It is important to know this but Rainmakers feel this information is useless in isolation.

Imagine you are in the middle of a deal. The client has made clear their pain and the areas you could add real value to them. You can then rank these areas of concern by order of importance. You also know who your competitor is. What if key areas of importance to the customer are areas in which your company doesn't do very well, but your competitor does? What do you do? Do you walk away from the deal? Whether you answer the last question or not, many salespeople do not even know that such a situation may arise in a deal. Do you know that one might analyse the competition in one deal, get an outcome, then analyse the same competition in another deal, and get a *different* outcome? This is because the variance between you and the competition is relative to what that particular customer wants out of that particular deal.

Rainmakers see the importance of analysing the competition on a deal-by-deal basis, depending on what is important to the customer. A Rainmaker will not hesitate for a split second to walk away if he knew his company was at a disadvantage during the deal. You can't win them all but you can win those that are yours for the taking.

> Remember:
> Choose
> where and
> how you
> fight.

Insight 146

Refracting the Competition

It's a known thing that you should never attack the competition. If you slate other companies during the sales process, it could seriously affect your chances of getting the deal. Well this is true… *to a point.*

Question: What if the prospect *asks* you how you compare to the competition, particularly if they are the incumbent?

Though one should never volunteer information about *the other side*, the Rainmaker is always ready and comfortable discussing the competition. It's not talking about them that is the issue, it's *what you say* that counts.

In my experience, the best way of talking about the competition is to focus on their weaknesses in generic terms and engineer the response so you are really talking about your company's *strengths* in the conversation.

Here is a scenario:

Prospect: How do you compare to Company B, who as you know are our current supplier?

Rainmaker: There are a number of differences between a large company and a smaller company. As a smaller company, we are able to provide a more personal service and we can respond to you very quickly. As a company becomes larger, it can become increasingly difficult to do that, instead of being 1 of 100 customers you are now 1 of 10,000 customers. We are able to provide all our services in-house rather than sub-contracting these core aspects, and our customers tend to remain loyal to us because of our can-do attitude. Would these attributes be the things you are interested in finding out more?

By responding in such a way, you will be attacking the competition but through the lens of your own strengths which demonstrates a high level of professionalism. In order to do this properly, you need to know the competition inside out, particularly their strengths and weakness. Perform a SWOT analysis of all your direct and indirect competitors, do the same for your own firm, and compare them all. This exercise will force you to understand how you interrelate in your market ecosystem.

> # Remember: Never be afraid to use the competition to make you look good.

Insight 147

Is Goal Hanging Really a Strategy?

When is a deal really a deal? When you get to receive the order? When the signed contracts come through? One would say yes. That is indeed when the fat lady actually sings. At this point, you can sit back and bask in the glory created by the success of your hard work. Until this point however, a deal is not a deal. Interestingly, this is also the case with the deals of our competitors.

Some of the biggest highlights in my sales career have occurred on occasions towards the end of the sales process of a particular deal. All the indicators show that my competitor was likely to get the order and then through timing, ingenuity, innovation and many a time, sheer luck, I was able to snatch victory from the jaws of defeat and close the deal.

To pip at the post can appear to be a phenomenon associated more with luck than any particular coherent plan but Rainmakers know that swiping the deal from their competitors at the last minute can actually be used as a strategy and as a mind-set. If she has done her homework properly, the Rainmaker will never give up on a deal irrespective of how *bad* the outlook may be. She knows that one encounter, one meeting, one word can change everything. This is not empty hope, but faith—real and tangible faith. Faith in her ability, faith in the ever-changing nature of the sales process and faith in the competition miscalculating. Rainmakers who may initially appear like the runner-up in the deal, the second choice, will always adopt a strategy of setting up the pieces on the deal chessboard so that as soon as the competitor wobbles, the Rainmaker is swiftly in control, forging ahead and never looking back.

As a Rainmaker, you must adopt the winning attitude, especially when you feel like you are not winning. Equally, if you are the front-runner, don't get pipped at the post.

Remember: "He who is prudent and lies in wait for an enemy who is not, will be victorious." Sun Tzu, Art of War.

Insight 148

Collapetition

The word "competitive" is probably the most obvious adjective that one thinks about when looking at the sales game. Being competitive is expected in sales. Phrases like "there are no prizes for coming second" or "the number two is the number one of the losers" are constantly drummed into salespeople by their managers and peers. The thought of not hitting their quarterly number keeps salespeople all over the world chasing deals in a reactive fashion like a hamster chasing itself on the hamster wheel. Make no mistake, we exist in a hyper-competitive environment where we compete with international players, globalisation, new business models, alternative solutions and indecisive apathy, let alone other competitors. However, ethically harnessing our God-given competitive spirit to achieve our goals through creativity, learning, innovation and value generation encompassed by hard work is key to being a Rainmaker. So yes, being competitive is critical to achieving success. But competition is a complex dynamic which can be destructive on many levels as well as life-enhancing.

Rainmakers see competition differently. They realise that they exist in an interconnected world where determining their thoughts and actions through the lens of the other players in their industry only proves to be counter-productive. Rainmakers realise that though they are in a competitive environment to win deals, they would rather focus on driving up value for customers, even if it involves working *with* traditional competitors to achieve positive and constructive outcomes for the customer. They "compete" but in a collaborative fashion where possible. Rainmakers work with all sorts of parties to solve problems for customers and if sometimes that has to be another industry player then so be it. Rainmakers on this level rarely see competition in the traditional sense. Rainmakers do battle with competition all the time but not in the way you think. Entrepreneur James Altucher put it aptly when he stated, "Your competition is not other people but the time you kill, the ill will you create, the knowledge you neglect to learn, the connections you fail to build, the health you sacrifice along the path, your inability to generate ideas, the people around you who don't support and love your efforts…"

Competing to win is normally a lifelong fight within you. Conquer that fight and you will achieve your goals without ever going to war.

> # Remember: Use all your resources to compete against the deserved competitor for the benefit of the customer and ultimately, your goals.

Insight 149

The Win-Lose Paradox

There are only four possible outcomes to any deal:

You win/they lose
You force onto them products or services they don't want or need and you bag a whole load of commission. That may be great for you financially in the short term but as you have added no value, your long-term relationship evaporates and so will your reputation.

You lose/they win
Due to a lack of the right skills and experience, you close a deal with little for your firm: little margin (if any), poor financial terms and difficult fulfilment deadlines. This will only create an environment of patchy service and at best, a problematic longer-term relationship.

You lose/they lose
There is no relationship. This may have been sabotaged earlier on in the sales process for whatever reason or the salesperson is trying to build a relationship with the wrong contact.

You win/they win
A fruitful business relationship. Symbiosis. Customer and Rainmaker working together to solve problems and enhance

business processes through trust and mutual understanding. My win-win formula looks like this:

Rainmaker value + your products/services = revenue (immediate and residual) + healthy margins + solid repeatable commissions

The Rainmaker value (RV) is really down to you and it is what has the biggest weighting on your side of the equation.

Ask yourself...really ask yourself:

- What am I doing to strive for win-win?

- How do I qualify and *pick* my clients?

- How can I add value to *all* the individuals within an account?

- How can I work smarter for the benefit of my clients?

- How do I create a scenario where I have *fewer* clients that I can focus on that bring in *more* good business?

- How can I demonstrate that I care about my customers' business and future?

> # Remember: Who dares wins, but who cares win-wins!

Insight 150

Time to Follow Up

Salespeople believe they are good at many things, particularly things that involve being "in theatre" such as face-to-face meetings, closing and negotiating. There are, however, key things that if done right, really help things along. One of those things is the *follow-up*. Following up is one of the easiest tasks to overlook or to procrastinate on, yet it is probably the biggest "glue" that binds the various fragments of the sales process together. Rainmakers understand a much-misunderstood concept of the follow-up and that is *timing*.

Stating at customer meetings and on the telephone exactly what the state of play is as well as the mutual points of agreement, then promptly following that up with an email thanking them for their time and restating what was discussed can go a long way towards demonstrating your character and integrity in the client's mind. Rainmakers do this quickly, elegantly, concisely and in accurate detail. Leave it too late and it loses not just its own fizz but also probably the fizz of the whole deal.

What is even more impressive to prospects, particularly on initial contact, is informing them exactly how and when you intend to follow up and actually seeing it through with military precision. Unbelievably, decision-makers are more used to salespeople *not bothering* to follow up rather than taking the time to make contact, outlining what was discussed and detailing action plans with timelines.

Rainmakers also find ways to follow up on their existing clients from time to time by being innovative and finding things of value to share with them. It could be an article that may be of interest to them or an idea that you feel will add value to their business in some way. By continually finding ways to follow up on your customer, you will keep the dialogue up, move the sales process along and grow the relationship.

> # Remember: If you have to wait for your customer to follow up on you, you will soon find your competition will be following up on them.

Insight 151

Radio Silence

Have you ever had a situation where you have presented a complete solution to the customer? They seem to agree with everything you say. But then, nothing. They don't get back to you, and they seem to not want to respond to your calls or emails. Only for a competitor to announce that they have won the deal.

One could come up with a number of reasons for this: the wrong solution, the wrong process, even the wrong salesperson. One major cause for this is *"the fit"*, or more pertinently, the lack of it. The problem here is that if the prospect doesn't feel that your solution fits *all* the parameters important to them then a deal will never really be on the table. The parameters may go beyond the usual commercial and technical ones. There may be political or even social considerations to take into account. As most prospects don't actually give you full feedback throughout the sales process, one could be in the dark and remain so, whilst thinking all is well.

The focus here is to qualify all the time *and* to gain agreement at every stage during the process. Trust your instincts and always cover all the bases.

If you still have radio silence, then contact the prospect stating you are "withdrawing" the proposal on the table and that you'll like to meet to discuss the solution again. Your intent is to either have a perfect fit on all levels or no fit at all.

Remember:
First
determine
the shape
of the hole
before
providing the
right peg.

Insight 152

Botheration

You know when you have those frustrating moments when the client seems really keen on a deal—you've uncovered the areas of need, written out a proposal and presented it to the client who has duly acknowledged it. Then things go quiet and you feel need to contact the client, but you don't want to come across as a pest? We all have those moments. There are two things to consider here.

Firstly, when you're initially in dialogue with the client, map out with them exactly how things would proceed once the proposal has gone in. What he/she/they would do and what you would do. Inform the prospect that you would be contacting them from time to time and ask whether that would be OK.

Secondly, when contacting the client, have a reason that would add value to their situation. Whether via email or phone, give the prospect another thing to consider. It may be a new statistic worth noting, a new methodology within that area, news of something that highlights your solution in a better light. Adding value through communication only serves to make the customer trust you more, as well giving you the opportunity to uncover more objections regarding the deal at hand.

Remember:
If you're not
in dialogue
with your
client, your
competitor
surely will
be.

Insight 153

"I have Only One Concern...or Maybe Two"

Salespeople tend to hate objections. When a prospect questions our price or quality or gives an excuse for not wanting to move forward, salespeople tend to see that as a hurdle that they unfortunately have to jump over...grudgingly!

Rainmakers, on the other hand, see objections in the sales process as *opportunities*. When a prospect begins to object to our product or service, they are really beginning to psychologically *evaluate* the solution, not resist it. That evaluation naturally brings up questions that need answering. This is a great place to be. Why? Because you have a chance to demonstrate to the customer that you are willing to dig deeper to understand their concerns and to *create value* by finding solutions to their particular issues. When a customer objects, I suggest you do the following:

- **Listen carefully**: let the prospect fully state their objection.

- **Empathise**: show you fully appreciate the prospect's concerns.

- **Qualify the objection**: ask why the prospect has these concerns, understand the drivers which get to the real heart of the issue.

- **Listen carefully:** let the prospect respond. Practise active listening.

- **Address Concerns:** look for innovative but realistic ways to address all their concerns.

- **Pre-close/Close:** once the concerns are addressed, seek to close or conditionally pre-close the prospect. If they raise another objection, go through this process again.

> # Remember:
> # A prospect
> # with no
> # concerns is
> # either buying
> # or lying.

Insight 154

Who's Teasing Who?

Face-time with prospective users and influencers is important. Face-time with decision-makers is particularly precious in the third quarter of the sales process. This is the period where the prospect or customer is evaluating the options. What are these options? *You and the competition*. What you do during this period is critical to the successful outcome of the deal.

In an i*deal* world, the decision-maker(s) would simply state a list of truthful objections that you would overcome one by one, so that everyone would be clear, a pragmatic evaluation would be made, a fair decision would be reached, and that would be that. However, decision-making in the corporate world is far from ideal.

Here is a rule of thumb for you: *for every objection the prospect has stated, there will be another one lurking that they may or may not be aware of, but will surely come to the fore in your absence, which could count against you.*

Just as a master watchmaker teases out a jewel from one of his timepieces, the Rainmaker teases out *points of clarification (PoC)*. I don't like using the word *objection* because it has negative connotations. It portrays resistance from the client, almost as if they are objecting to your solution, your company and you. PoC, however, is a positive term. It shows that the customer may not be clear on certain areas particularly relative to the competition. A Rainmaker, therefore, will always want to look for these points to create and maintain absolute clarity.

Rainmakers have no choice but to control as much as possible during the all-important face-time with decision-makers. As usual, the method of control is questions. Use questions to search for PoCs. Once you are approaching the end of the meeting, don't rely on the proverbial "Is there anything else?" Use assumptive questions that start with "let's assume for a minute that…", or "Imagine if you will that…". I sometimes use the 1-10 scenario—i.e. "How, between 1-10, would you rate this solution against our competitors?" and based on the answer: "What are the areas we can look at together that will help us to get to a 10 in your estimation?" These are simple tools Rainmakers use to tease out the PoCs that otherwise may only have been dealt with by the competition. Seek out, study and practise ways to tease out PoCs and you will put yourself in a much better position for the final home stretch of the sales process—the Decision.

> # Remember: Always ask yourself: Who's teasing who?

Insight 155

A Priceless Deal

Here is a frustrating scenario that can happen to any of us. You are working on a large opportunity, the sales process is progressing smoothly, and you seem to have so far covered all the bases. The solution is technically advanced; the value added fits a particular set of requirements; you have identified and influenced all the main users, influencers and decision-makers; the price is competitive and the budget has been approved. All of a sudden, they inform you that your price is too high and that you have to make significant reductions. You do, only to find that you lose the deal, or in some cases, you do not move on price—again, only to find out you lose the deal. It seems you are in trouble whether you move on price or not. This is a classic case of the customer using price as a red herring.

The Rainmaker is always conscious of the fact that the final stages of the sales cycle are the most crucial time to keep antennae up and stay tuned into what is going on. They know that once internal and informal decisions are made, it is almost impossible to reverse them. Rainmakers know that sometimes, customers make decisions for the most frivolous of reasons and then use price as a mechanism to get the salesperson to engineer his or her own exit from the process.

Towards the latter stages of a deal, it is paramount to seek out and understand the points of clarification required about you, your company and your solutions. If the customer brings to your attention an issue such as price, find out what the *real* concerns are, no matter how fickle they may be. This stage of the deal is where you should be up close and personal with your insider. However, the quality of the information you obtain from your insider will only be as good as the quality of the questions you ask. If you are genuinely in a negotiating situation, it would be prudent to find out all the parameters that you are working with and the position that you are negotiating from, so that if you indeed have to make concessions, you get something in return as well as the desired effect: *the order.*

Remember: The Rainmaker uses experience and a sharp eye to see beyond the smokescreen of price.

Insight 156

Negative

"Have the courage to say NO. Have the courage to face the truth. Do the right thing because it is right. These are the magic keys to living your life with integrity". That's what W. Clement Stone once said. It's a nice quotation but in practice saying NO can be hard.

The thing is that saying NO at the right time in the right way can actually be integral to building powerful business relationships with your prospects and clients. The true relationship between the Rainmaker and his customer can only be based on mutual respect and trust. Both of these important qualities won't develop if you can't say NO when you believe it is truly in the interest of the client.

The problem is that most of our behavioural weaknesses stem from our childhood experiences. The "no factor" is one of those weaknesses. We have always associated NO with something negative—or indeed dangerous—as our parents would say an emphatic no to anything that may potential cause us harm as children. Therefore, saying NO to a prospect can create a double psychological effect where you would subconsciously think *they* would respond to the no factor negatively.

So here we are, trying to use a negative word to create a positive relationship. The trick here is the *timing* and *how* you say NO. Saying NO should always be a part of a larger quest to be congruent in everything you do—that is, being internally and externally consistent with your principles. If you are clear on what is always in the best interests of your customer, if a difference in opinion arises, it's down to you to demonstrate your ability as the customer's "trusted advisor" that you know your stuff and are not afraid to advise accordingly even if that means saying NO and walking away.

The days of doing anything for an order are long gone. Rainmakers slowly build longer-term consultative relationships founded on mutual trust and respect and not necessarily familiarity.

> Remember: If the relationship is worth its weight in commissions, saying "no" now will invariably lead to a "yes" in the future.

Insight 157

ABC

Many of us recall the "sales" movie, *Glengarry Glen Ross*, an on-screen adaptation of the 1984 Pulitzer Prize-winning play of the same name. The film's most famous—and indeed poignant—scene was the "pep talk" the character referred to as "Blake" (played by Alec Baldwin) delivers to an underperforming sales team of a land real estate firm. The scene, which wasn't part of the original play, runs for around eight minutes and can be blood-curdling to watch. What was meant to be a motivational speech was inspirational to the sales team...if you're inspired to run to a dark corner and sob! That is why some of the principles marshalled out by Blake in that scene get a bad rap these days. One of those principles is *ABC—Always Be Closing!*

This basic principle in the world of sales is still seen as part of the old order of selling, where one uses high-pressure tactics to close deals in a purely transactional environment. The thinking is that if you repeat the close often enough and hard enough, the prospect will eventually wilt under the pressure and buy! This indeed did happen and still does today, but selling without ethics is *not* Rainmaking.

However, consider this: getting people, companies, or internal departments to buy a product or service that is of real value to them only happens in steps. On many occasions, these steps are very small. It could be getting the prospect to agree to a first meeting over coffee, or agreeing to look through a detailed proposal, or to coach you on the internal power structure within their organisation. There are so many complex routes the Rainmaker must navigate to successfully arrive at the order. These steps involve helping people to make decisions and to gain agreement along the way. These small steps must be closed every time for the Rainmaker to move forward. Lots of "little closes" will invariably lead to the big close!

Therefore, Rainmakers *are* always closing, always gently pushing for small steps of agreement on the way to the deal being finalised, and even then, the closing never stops. Do what Rainmakers do: Always be closing!

> # Remember: Small agreements earlier on lead to large orders further down the line.

Insight 158

Phantom of the Opera

On the 25th of May 1965 in Maine, Massachusetts, Mohammad Ali finally beat Sonny Liston to become the heavyweight boxing champion of the world. Because it was a rematch after a controversial earlier fight, this fight happened in a remote part of Massachusetts as opposed to Boston. Therefore, only 2,434 fans could attend. Yet none of these fans actually saw the first round knockout blow that felled Sonny Liston. To this day, the punch is known as the *Phantom Punch*. Ali later said: "I hit him so quickly, no one ever saw it!" Liston and the fans didn't see Ali coming. Everyone underestimated him and he took the title and began a long and interesting career as "*The Champ*".

One of the most significant stages in the sales process is the *close*. Sometimes it's a grand boardroom event where you convince the decision-makers to commit, or it could happen very quickly on the phone or via email. As a Rainmaker, you always have to be prepared to close — however you don't always want to come across as a closer. Nobody likes being closed, but everyone likes making a positive decision. It's the Rainmaker's job to help make that positive decision to commit a seamless and enjoyable one. Focus on the *experience* of the decision rather than the decision itself. The decision should be the by-product of the experience. This way, they never see you coming. They never see the *Phantom Close*.

Remember:
Let your
prospects
see their
decision,
not your
close!

Insight 159

Close the Deal Without a Fight

In the late 6ᵗʰ century BC, Sun Tzu authored the work *The Art of War*. The book went on to become one of the world's oldest and indeed most successful books on military strategy. Sun Tzu begins the book by stating the following:

"The art of war is of vital importance to the state. It is a matter of life or death, a road to either safety or ruin. Hence under no circumstances can it be neglected". In the context of selling, this statement can be used as a metaphor for what we do.

Here is my revision of that statement:

"*The art of Making Rain is of vital importance to one's wellbeing. It's a matter of boom or bust, a road to a good life and fulfilment or no work and penniless existence. Therefore under no circumstances can it be neglected*".

Ok, I know it's a bit overdramatic, but the point here is that as the Chinese undertook their military campaigns from a strategic context, we as Rainmakers should do likewise with our business, accounts and *competitors*. Here are some of my tips from the book:

- **Think strategy:** Take a strategic view of what you do and how you need to achieve the results.

- **Know yourself:** Stop and think periodically about your strengths and weaknesses and how far you are going to enhance the former and overcome the latter.

- **Know your competition:** Find out who you are up against. Look for the strengths and weaknesses of the company and if possible the individual salesperson.

- **Know your prospect:** Find out everything about their business, issues, environment, strengths and weaknesses.

- **View competition as positioning:** Your job in the sales process is like a chess master. You are not really "fighting" your competitor as much as *making moves and counter moves* that force them to move. That in itself *is the essence of the art.*

- **Be formless:** Find connections to different people within the prospect's organisation. In this case, *be all things to all men.* Financial people, technical people, management, users. At the very least, tie them up with similar people within your company. This way, you have a web of connections that will influence the ultimate buyer(s).

> Remember: For the Rainmaker, every day is war and the prize is peace and prosperity.

Insight 160

Brünnhilde's Aria

August 1876 saw the premiere of the last of Richard Wagner's four operas (*Der Ring des Nibelungen*) entitled *Götterdämmerung*. The opera is of a grand nature and typically features buxom sopranos. The notable piece is the final aria performed by the character *the Valkyrie Brünnhilde*. This solo marks the very end of the performance.

Brünnhilde's aria subsequently inspired the writer and broadcaster Dan Cook after the first basketball game in 1978 between NBA's San Antonio Spurs and Washington Bullets. Cook stated: "The opera ain't over till the fat lady sings". This is a mantra that is so prevalent and true in sports. It is also true in the sport of selling.

There are many decisions, actions and events that take place during the selling process. Securing that all-important meeting, finally being invited to tender, being selected to the final stage, getting the "nod", being given the platform to convince the board, and so on. The Rainmaker, however, understands that none of these developments matter if the signed order with a corresponding order number does not come through—and even then Rainmakers see that as simply the penultimate round. The signed contract *is* Brünnhilde's aria. Without these documents finally emerging, the deal potentially can be snatched from under you for a myriad of reasons, least of all the competition.

Progress is the only way through the buying cycle but one must always keep their eyes on the prize and diligently work through the process covering all bases until the fat lady truly does sing.

Remember:
It's not
over
till it's
over.

Insight 161

Agree to Agree

People talk about negotiating all the time. It seems to be a skill boasted about frequently but rarely exercised effectively. To Rainmakers, proper negotiation skills are vital to achieving higher revenue, more profitability and the best possible terms on a deal. Rainmakers use negotiation to make deals favourable to both parties and not simply react to how the prospect wants the deal to pan out.

Negotiation is really about power. Outlined below are seven potential sources of that power:

- **Quid Pro Quo:** Never offer anything until they have offered you something first.

- **Options:** The more options your solutions and services have (over your competition) in creating value to the potential client, the less of an alternative the prospect will have in selecting others, thus the more negotiating power you will possess.

- **No Cash:** Offer anything but a direct discount, as a discount is raw cash off your company's top line revenue and margins. Whatever alternatives you do offer, make sure the perceived value is equal to the discount value the customer seeks.

- **Time:** If the prospect is running to a tight deadline, you will have more leverage to negotiate.

- **Relationship:** Right from the word go, you need to be developing your relationship based on mutual respect with the various players in the account, as it will be from the strength of these relationships that some of your negotiating advantage will come.

- **Investment:** How much time and energy has the customer put into the buying process? If you recognise that over the sales cycle and the prospect has really worked hard with you on this, there will then certainly be room to negotiate at the end of the process.

- **Credibility:** The credibility of YOU is what you are really selling. The more credible the prospect sees you, the easier it will be to set out favourable terms.

- **Knowledge:** Sir Francis Bacon stated in 1597 that *knowledge is power*. This directly applies here. The more knowledge you have of your customer's issues, organisation, goals, timelines and most importantly, their needs, the more you will find opportunities to negotiate.

- **Skill:** Nobody is born a negotiator! It's a learned skill. The only way you can learn an important skill is by studying, modelling and practising. In the end, all skills are about three words. Practice, practice and practice.

Remember: Negotiating is about take and give, not give and take.

Insight 162

The After Party

When is it most critical to give an account the most attention? When prospecting? When trying to get the deal? When asking for the order?

In an ideal world it'll be all the time. But the period in which it is most crucial to give the client that extra focus is *just after they have raised the order!* When an order is raised, an interesting thing happens:

From the client's side, they would have gone through a selection process of some sort and eventually decided upon you. Therefore, they want to feel like they have made the *right* choice based on the subsequent chain of events after the order is raised.

However, from your side, now you have the order you can relax and start focusing your mind on the *next* deal to close, thus taking your eye of the ball somewhat and hoping project management or customer services might sort things out.

These two scenarios are definitely at odds with one another and ultimately, customer service suffers and trust gets dented even before the project is up and running.

Rainmakers don't just manage the account but also the *dynamic* of the account—that is to say, the customer's experience throughout the cycle especially the days and weeks after the order has been raised.

Remember: What keeps your firm alive is the "lifetime value" of the customer, not the first order.

Insight 163

Mind Your Own Business

The standard school of thought in selling is that the end of the sales cycle is the close. Once you have closed the deal, the only thing you have to think about is getting referrals. This may be the case in the transactional selling environment, but Rainmakers sell consultatively. They look at the bigger picture. They are in it for the long haul. The term to take note of here is "sales cycle"—once you win a deal, the cycle within the account has only just begun.

As a rainmaker, your calling card is value. Everything about what you do, what you sell and what your firm does is about adding value to your customer. Therefore, when the customer commits to going with your firm, your job at that point is to *orchestrate the realisation of that value* which up to that point has been just a potential, locked in with the sales cycle. YOU are the champion of the customer within your company, which means that though you may work with designers, project managers, product specialists, installers, etc., your job is to manage them on behalf of the customer. You are required to project-manage the "moments of truth" that the customer are likely to experience with all facets of your firm. Once your client realises this, they become a client for the long term.

The point here is that you need to see this business as your business. That is, you are the CEO of your business and thus it'll be your responsibility to oversee and manage all aspects of your business. See your business as a *franchise* operation connected to the main business. If you do things right, your business will grow and so will your income. Conversely, if you don't take responsibility and manage your business, then your franchise will be stagnate and even decline, which would be of no use to the business as a whole.

Rainmakers are first and foremost entrepreneurs, so take steps to start thinking, behaving and managing like one.

> # Remember: Value your business by helping your clients fully realise the value of theirs.

Insight 164

Happiness, Shared

There are only two ways to hit and exceed your targets. By being lucky or by having a large sales pipeline. If you are relying on the former, one day your luck may just run out. To be consistently on top of your targets year on year you must always have a large pipeline. A proportion of your time *every day* should be devoted to getting brand new business. There are numerous ways to do this such as cold calling, marketing campaigns, seminars and trade shows.

One simple method that possesses a high hit rate is *asking for referrals*. It's that simple, but funnily enough, we never seem to take the time to do it and do it properly.

Think of the customer that you sold to last. He or she is part of a network of similar professionals, including friends, colleagues that have moved on, business partners and even their competitors. They all are part of a group that you can easily tap into by harnessing the power of referrals.

When I log onto LinkedIn, there is a section that informs me on how big my "network" actually is. You can have 100 contacts and your *total network* is over 5,000 strong. Now that is what I call the compound effect. Billion-dollar multi-level marketing companies like Amway and Mary Kay Cosmetics understand the compounding power of referrals so well that it forms the foundation of their business models.

Imagine how much potential business can come your way if you use proper referral techniques. Read up on it, learn it and practise it.

> # Remember: Rainmakers build their businesses by just asking again and again.

Insight 165

David's Question

David was my very first mentor and coach. I started out in sales fresh out of university with bags of enthusiasm and passion but less of an understanding of what I was really getting myself into (I think naivety is the word). David helped softened the shocks of the reality of industry, commerce and the selling game. One day, over one of our numerous coffee chats, I noticed David began to stare at his freshly made latte with the furrows on his forehead beginning to deepen and I knew he was about to get all philosophical on me. "Jonas, I'm going to ask you a rhetorical question".

"Here we go", I told myself, smiling. "Why rhetorical?" I quizzed.

"Because rhetorical questions exist to make you think, man!" David quipped with a slight irritation lingering in his voice.

"OK, fire away," I sighed.

"What is the difference between a customer and a client? If you manage to understand and embody the answer to my question, then you will do well in this game".

I remember saying to myself initially that that was hardly a question that warranted "rhetorical" status. I thought that there was only so much philosophy one could squeeze from such a question. "Of course I know the answer" I told myself at the time, somewhat disappointed after such a build-up. That was almost 20 years ago. Over the years, the more I thought about the question, the less obvious the answer seemed. But then I came across another question that gave me my eureka moment. What is the difference between repeat business and loyal business? The answer to that is simple. Repeat business is where the customer makes a rational decision to buy from you and continue to buy from you. On the face of it, that seems OK, right? The only problem is that if your competitor comes up with a better solution, a cheaper offering, a more compelling story, then the shift to your competitor will be swift. Even if you have service level agreements, lock in clauses, or other guarantees of keeping their business, if a customer wants to move, they will. In today's business environment, customer loyalty appears to be a distant notion. However, loyal business is where the *client* makes an *emotional* decision to buy from you and continue to buy from you whatever happens, whether your prices go up, or technically better products come onto the market, or during a recession; whatever the situation, your client will be loyal to you. Why? Because they believe what you and your company believe. They have not just connected with what you do but why you do what you do! You both share values and therefore they have invested in you and your company with something money cannot transact— emotion. That's the difference between clients and customers.

Salespeople look for customers they can transact with; Rainmakers seek out clients they can develop deep personal and corporate relationships with on many levels. Relationships that involve mutual value, trust, respect and integrity. This is Rainmaking. Mutual investment between two parties: You and the client.

> Remember: Venture beyond the transactional into the emotional.

Insight 166

David's Question II

David's Question centred around loyalty which is an interesting concept. There was a time when much of the business strategy of the first head of IBM, Thomas J. Watson, was centred on developing and maintaining customer loyalty through purely sales tactics. That worked in the early-to-late 20th century. Now, with the proliferation of competition (direct and indirect), the growth of the web and the internal pressures customers face daily—loyalty is dead...*or is it?*

The reality is this: customers do not seek loyalty they seek value. If they find value, real value, they will remain loyal. Warning: Regardless of the relationship, if the value remains static, they will move on to the value-proposing competitor in a heartbeat!

This phenomenon is a double-edged sword and Rainmakers take advantage of one side of the sword and avoid the other. On one hand, you can benefit from the lack of loyalty to take business from your competitors and on the other hand use value to keep competitors out. What Rainmakers find is that grabbing customers is much easier than holding on to them and that the watch phrase here is *value, always value.*

Consistently and *exponentially* demonstrating value through ideas, concepts, solutions, delivery and YOU, as well as developing *deep* relationships based on mutual respect with key individuals in the account will foster loyalty and increase the lifetime commercial net worth of the customer.

Remember:
There are no
real sales
results until
you achieve
customer
loyalty.

Insight 167

A Basic Survival Tool

In the insight, *"Your Most Prized Possession"*, I used the hip-hop phrase "Word is Bond" to illustrate how important keeping your promises are. Well here is another hip-hop phrase: *"Street Cred"*. Just like keep your word, having street cred—or indeed, an *earned respect*—can prolong your life on the mean streets of New York City and ultimately make you successful.

A Rainmaker has to be credible. Unlike those on the streets of NYC that build up a reputation over years, Rainmakers have to build their credibility all over again every day with a new prospect, client or contact.

The word *credibility* comes from the Latin word credo which literally means *"I believe"*. The fact is simple: You need to be believable to influence and you need to influence to make rain. Here are ten quick pointers to establish credibility with your prospects:

1. Study the experts to be an expert.

2. Focus your thoughts, time and resources on value.

3. Prepare! Prepare!! Prepare!!!

4. Word is Bond.

5. Diligently seek out and get to know all contacts in the account (especially the *scary* ones).

6. Actively listen (you have two ears and one mouth).

7. Take full responsibility of *all* your actions.

8. Be comfortable with who you are, what you do and what (and how) you sell.

9. "Equalise" the relationships with your contacts. Think Parity.

10. Have the courage to say NO if it's in everyone's best interest (you must always seek win-win).

Credibility is like an organism that can grow and form a life of its own. It can follow you as well as lead the way for you. Create it, develop it, build it, protect it and most importantly use it!

> # Remember: The street cred you create when you are there sells you when you're not.

Insight 168

When Death is Welcome

Jerry Seinfeld, during one of his stand-up routines, said, "According to most studies, people's number one fear is public speaking. Number two is death. Death is number two. Does that seem right? That means to the average person, if you have to go to a funeral, you're better off in the casket than doing the eulogy".

On the one hand, I'm not sure if you would feel the same way if death was staring you in the face about to pounce, but on the other hand, if the majority of people are scared of presenting, then chances are your competitors are too.

Whichever way you look at it, Rainmakers *must* present solutions, ideas, concepts, plans and analysis. Rainmakers must use their presentation skills to influence decision-makers.

Yes, you have to do things like practice and learn how to manage your nerves. However, in my experience, there are two things that can turn you into a superstar presenter.

- **Develop a multi-dimensional expertise:** If you are clear about what you are presenting and why, and you know the subject inside out, then presenting will simply become a natural expression of what you already know. It'll be like explaining to a bunch of school kids what a car is.

- **Have the right attitude:** All the best presenters out there love what they do, they are passionate about what they are saying and it shows. Being fervent about who you are and what you're trying to convey will only give you the *self-confidence* to see you through.

If you love skiing, for example, and you had to present on your skiing skills and adventures, you would do it exceedingly well because you know about the topic like the back of your hand *and* you would be passionate about it.

Remember: The only death you should welcome is the death of fear.

Insight 169

The Bill, Please...

In Oliver Stone's 1987 film *Wall Street*, Gordon Gekko famously states "Lunch is for wimps". I guess watching the salespeople who always seem to dash out to lunch when the internal school bell rings, he might just have a point. However, Rainmakers recognise that *taking clients out to lunch* can be a way of accelerating the sales process if done properly, particularly within the fourth quarter of the sales cycle.

Some of the biggest deals have been closed in a bar or restaurant. Why? Because with all the politics, pressure and wandering eyes, the office is actually not the prospect's comfort zone. Take the prospect out of there and you have an environment conducive for conducting business through the lens of personal engagement.

To make a lunch meeting really profitable, the trick is to know what you want to achieve from the encounter and to always be in control. Here are some tips to that end:

- Never suggest lunch just because you can. All engagements with a prospect or customer are deadly serious and should have a specific objective.

- Always have a clear outcome determined in your mind from the lunch, be it a pre-close, close, referral, coaching for a big presentation or for fact-finding.

- Thoroughly prepare for lunch like any other meeting.

- Chose the venue and use this opportunity to impress the client. If the restaurant is near you, pop in beforehand and discuss your requirements with the staff. Sometimes you can go as far as instructing the waiter to welcome you and remember your name.

- If possible, make the client sit facing just you with nothing behind you. This way the client can only give YOU their full attention with no distractions over your shoulder.

- You are not there to drastically deplete your expense account and feast out. Order something light but decent for yourself. This will enable you to stay alert and focus on the task at hand.

- Be brief. Though you are in control, the prospect's time is always limited.

- Remember, you are also out of an office environment. Always maintain an air of professionalism about you. Don't fall into the trap of over-familiarity.

- Relax. Lunch is business but in a far more relaxed way.

As a Rainmaker, you should always know that taking prospects out to lunch is a *strategic tool* that should be used to progress and speed up the sales cycle. But like a "get out of jail free card", you can only effectively use this tool sparingly.

Remember:
Eat the
good food
but sow the
good seed
to reap
the good
rewards.

Insight 170

We Are All In This Together

We all know of John Donne's classic quotation: "No man is an island". We all need a support network in our personal lives, social lives and most definitely in our sales careers. In terms of the latter, one may see support as technical support from the professional services team, management support or indeed support from other colleagues and even clients.

Question: What support provides the highest value to a Rainmaker?

Answer: *Other Rainmakers.*

Historically, selling has always been a lonely, selfish game. You, the individual, are given an individual target and are solely responsible for that target. With a bit of training coupled with technical and management support, off you go and don't come back till you have orders. However, the business ecosystem is forever dynamic and currently, from a macro perspective, emerging countries (such as Goldman Sachs' BRIC nations) are redefining global markets, capital projects are increasing and becoming exclusively larger, while funds are becoming scarcer in the mature economies such as the UK. In addition, from a micro perspective, customers are less loyal, they are consistently demanding more *tangible value* from whomever can deliver—the sales process is becoming increasingly harder to predict.

In the face of all these challenges however lie opportunities for great rewards if we think outside the box and innovate. One way to do that is to sell as a team.

What then does this actually mean? It's simply utilising the resources of individual Rainmakers to continually raise the knowledge and experience capital of the entire group of Rainmakers.

This all starts with the whole team developing a personal and corporate mind-set of *"we are all in this together"*. Curiously, the following can happen:

- Rainmakers will begin to share their experiences of their customers, prospects, lost deals, competitors and other suppliers.

- Rainmakers will share new information on products, innovations, market changes, relevant news, etc.

- Rainmakers begin to exchange opportunities that best fit the Rainmaker and expect the same to be done in return.

By focusing on and excelling at these points, Rainmakers (as a team and as individuals) will win in the face of these interesting times.

> # Remember: More Rainmakers, more rain!

Insight 171

Old Enemies, New Friends

Marketing. Ah yes! A concept heard and spoken a lot in the sales arena. A concept also poorly understood yet vital to our sales effort, our targets, our commissions. Peter F. Drucker, the "Father of modern management", once stated: "The aim of marketing is to know and understand the customer so well the product or service fits him and sells itself". Drucker's point is simple: good marketing makes the Rainmaker's job easier and more enjoyable.

Though sales and marketing are quite different, their goals are exactly the same: More revenue and margin. *Marketing creates the conditions that increase the interactions between prospects and the business. Sales turns those interactions into business.*

The magic of both these processes is created when both functions work in harmony towards the goal. The Rainmaker knows that working closely with marketing can increase her revenue. How? By understanding the marketing *cold face* of advertising, promotions, public relations, product development, channel development and web-based activities, the Rainmaker gives and gains constant feedback about the whole business she is in and the *field* she plays the game in. Not only is that knowledge and insight invaluable, but one also increases the opportunity for gaining new contacts, new areas of business and new ways of doing deals. All of which adds to the bottom line.

The sales arena is constantly fluid. The rate of change is now moving exponentially. Markets rise and fall; industries undergo rapid and chronic metamorphosis. Marketing helps business to adapt commercially. The Rainmaker takes advantage of this. After all, one can sell the same way in a new environment and not achieve much.

Make the effort to understand the marketing role—particularly how it relates to you. Work closer with marketing both in your firm and in your suppliers' firms. Communicate with them about what your prospects and customers are saying and listen to their feedback. The sum total of this effort only serves to enrich you as a Rainmaker in more ways than one.

> Remember: Those who sell well do so through the works of those who market well and vice versa.

Insight 172

Outbreak

It's a fact of life that many companies still foster a destructive sales environment. When you bring a number of sensitive, driven and independently minded egos together it can, if left unchecked, create a culture that may ultimately become toxic. The negativity that comes from inexperienced managers, the wrong corporate culture, backstabbing colleagues or simply just unhealthy pursuit of profit without a vision and sense of purpose can infect a team leading to less revenue generated and profit realised.

Whatever the culture and environment, Rainmakers rise above the fray. They always see themselves running a business within a business. They value their franchise-like independence almost like a multi-level marketing representative. Therefore, they feel immune from the storms of company politics or the outbreak of toxicity.

I remember working for a large company that, looking back, was not really growing but consolidating as a group. There was a lot of negativity and in fighting at board level. This negativity spread down through the managers to the staff. It was particularly acute within the sales team. The sales managers were too inexperienced as people managers and leaders to keep the salespeople focused on the numbers. They had the salespeople follow activity-based metrics without an overall reason or purpose. Low morale and needless uncertainty pervaded the teams, which directly affected revenue. There was, however, one salesperson, one Rainmaker, who was not only focused on overachieving the numbers but was also benefiting from this sorry state of affairs by taking over the profitable accounts of people who resigned. I asked him whether all of this affected him he replied, "I run my own 'virtual' company and my ultimate bosses are my customers—they pay the company who in turn give me my cut, so irrespective of what is going on here, my *arrangement* with my real bosses suits me just fine".

This arrangement with the customers in this Rainmaker's mind was his anchor in amidst all the chaos. He used his anchor to form a protective barrier around his thinking and focus.

What is your anchor? How do you protect yourself from toxic attitudes and personalities that can come from anywhere?

As human beings we are social animals. The essence of our being and our survival throughout the ages have been based on group interaction and groupthink. Just as inspired positivity can make groups achieve the impossible, negativity can have a devastating effect on groups, be it families, communities, nations or sales teams. Recognising that fact and shielding yourself from negative energy whilst harnessing your own positive spirit by developing fortitude of mind and focusing on the real priorities will keep your career moving and your bank balance flowing.

> # Remember: Negativity is the polar opposite of creativity and excellence. The three cannot coexist.

Insight 173

Car Time

Learning forms the basis of being a Rainmaker. Understanding yourself, your profession, your industry and then putting things into practice is what propels you forward to Rainmaking success. This takes energy, commitment and *time*. The question arises though: With all the pressures on time in today's world, when can one find the time to study, to learn, to reflect, to understand? Hidden in the question lies the answer. One does not find time, one can only *make* time.

The more you manage yourself, the more you create time. The antonym for creating time is wasting time and if you look at your typical day through the eyes of a time management guru, you would be amazed at how much time you actually squander in a 24-hour period. Time that could be used accelerating your race to Rainmaking excellence and success.

One of the biggest time black holes is the time spent in the car, driving back and forth and up and down motorways trying to meet with clients and prospects. Sales professionals can spend more than four hours per working day in their cars. That is over a full working month sitting in the car every year. A whole calendar month! That's over 9% of the entire calendar year one is forced to sit and listen. This begs the question: What would be the best thing to listen to for 9% of the year if you thought about it pragmatically?

There is a concept that has been around in the US for a while now. It's called *University on Wheels*. This is simply deciding to use the time spent in cars to study in an area of expertise of your choice. Several websites stock downloadable audio books on virtually anything. If you look hard enough, you can even download free older audio books whose copyright is in the public domain, or you could simply buy the audio files. The point is you can spend time listening to lectures on anything. You can even make up your own. I sometimes record thoughts on my iPhone and play them back through the car speakers via Bluetooth just so that I can reinforce the thoughts in my mind. Imagine what you master by listening and learning about self-development, selling skills and technical information for 840 full hours in a working calendar year? You would be getting better at what you do, you would be more confident in your profession. The knowledge gained in that time can never be taken away from you. It's yours to keep, it's yours to build on. As the Chinese proverb goes: *"Learning is a treasure that will follow its owner everywhere"*.

> # Remember: Drive yourself forward whilst driving and you will never need the reverse gear.

Insight 174

Rainmaker + Technology = Extraordinary!

Whilst growing up, I loved Lee Majors in the 1970s ABC TV series *The Six Million Dollar Man*. Yes, he was a man trying to make his way in the world, but he had the advantage of science and technology to enable him to push the boundaries of what's humanly possible.

Technology can be defined as the application of scientific knowledge for practical purposes. Almost all disciplines use technology to achieve ends quicker and smarter. From medicine to manufacturing, from accounting to power generation—technology seems to be the cornerstone of advancement in the modern society of today. Selling has however always been a simple, straightforward process with more emphasis on personal skill than anything else. This, however, seems to be changing. Over the last 20 years technology has transformed the way one communicates with prospects and clients. The use of email, the Internet, multimedia, converging communication technologies and social media is enabling sales professionals to sell smarter.

Rainmakers are constantly on the lookout for new ways to leverage technology in order to continually add value to customers. They have no choice; things are moving so quickly that the competitor who proactively reacts with faster, smarter, slicker methods of getting the job done wins the day. The use of technology forms a large part of this. The interesting thing is that most of these technologies are actually at all of our fingertips—it's simply about the canny application of them. With social networking sites, smartphone apps, video conferencing and customer relationship management software all on your smartphone, you never have a reason not to respond to clients, get face-time or add value.

> Remember:
> Outsmart the
> competition with
> the tools available
> to you.

Insight 175

The Currency that Talks

Just imagine for a minute that the atmosphere is full of money. All around you are real $100 dollar bills. The only thing however, is that they are somewhat translucent and you have to train your eye to spot them. Not only that, but once you do spot them, you have to develop the technique of actually capturing them. You know that once you can train your eye's biconvex lens to *see* the money and train your hands to *grasp* it you will be rich beyond your wildest dreams.

The reality of this fantasy illustration can be summed up in a single word: Information.

It is said that *information is the currency of today's world*. The only way to become (and stay) rich is through information. It's the information the wealthy gain that is used to create jobs, profit, whole industries and markets. This in turn creates social and anthropological shifts which then spawn new information which can be picked up and the cycle continues. It never stops. Tapping into that cycle and responding to it creates wealth and the Rainmaker is acutely aware of this.

With the right information, one can make the right decisions, and with the right decisions, larger and more profitable deals can be closed. The Rainmaker is always aware that the lifeblood of any sales process is *information*. Rainmakers search for it, use it, protect it and sometimes even bargain with it. The information may be of a higher level such as where markets are going, or how customers are responding to those market shifts. It could be technological information and its implications for customers. It may also be micro information on a particular deal or customer.

The Native Americans used to place their ears to the ground to pick up the vibrations of horses' hooves to warn them of an impending attack. In the same vein, we all need to put our ears to the ground constantly to gain vital information. Whether it's through constantly developing new contacts, always talking to existing contacts, really listening to your customers, or staying on top of industry publications. The information out there is yours to harness and transform into knowledge, which you can turn into lots of very real $100 dollar bills.

Remember: The world favours the eagle-eyed and the enterprising hand.

Insight 176

Blog or Die!

Imagine a world in the not-too-distant future where recruiters of experienced salespeople will be stating that it's mandatory that you have a long-standing blog with a minimum of X'000 followers before they even consider you for an interview. Sounds far-fetched, right? Or does it? Let's consider the role of the salesperson in the buying process since I started in sales in 1997. In those days buyers used us to transact. Salespeople told buyers what was required and how much it was going to cost, negotiated the price and transacted the deal. We were like transaction facilitators. Post-2000, buyers approached salespeople for information on the products and solutions, then we would show them the features, advantages and benefits of the products and if our solution fit, we might close the deal. We were like information providers.

Today, with the proliferation of technology and communications, buyers use the Internet to buy commodity items without ever speaking to a salesperson. If buyers need specialist information they simply go online and find out, again, without the use of a salesperson. So how can salespeople add value to their customers and prospects today?

Rainmakers leverage the Internet to gain trust. Massive trust. If prospects trust and respect you, they are more likely to engage with you. If they have heard of you, they are more likely to take your call or respond to your email. You can gain trust and respect by one-to-one or one-to-some encounters with customers and prospects like meetings and presentations. However, Rainmakers go for one-to-millions by using the Internet. How do they do this? They blog.

By starting a blog, Rainmakers are able to build up a platform. It is this platform that constitutes the reservoir from which their pipeline grows. Through a blog, followers form opinions about the Rainmaker who in turn carefully controls what is put out there. Rainmakers know that content and consistency is key to a successful blog. Rainmakers only put out content that is 80% about life and 20% about the product, service or solution. They know that the trick is to make the solution relevant to real life within the content. Rainmakers also write frequently and consistently. Daily, weekly or bi-weekly, but without fail. Then they use as many social media platforms as possible to get the message out.

It's time to write a blog. You have no choice in the matter. You have to start to build your own platform and begin to mine it in order to stay in business. Research online how to start this, and be tomorrow's salesperson today.

> # Remember:
> # The bigger your platform, the more valuable you'll be.

Insight 177

Share Your Thoughts

Futurist and scenario-based strategist Daniel Ramus once said, "Thought leadership should be an entry point to a relationship. Thought leadership should intrigue, challenge, and inspire even people already familiar with a company. It should help start a relationship where none exists, and it should enhance existing relationships".

All salespeople who expect to be successful must become thought leaders in their field. Like blogging, there really isn't a choice in the matter.

The role of the salesperson has changed forever. Decision-makers are no longer looking for details on the product specification, the characteristics of the service offered or even how your company can help solve a particular problem. With the advent of the Internet and social media, information is everywhere. Customers are really looking for insight. They are searching for the *why*. A new perspective on their business, a left-field approach to a challenge, an innovative way of thinking and doing that produces better results than the norm, at a lower cost.

The Rainmaker stands out by providing this information and therefore gets the attention of prospects that competitors only dream of reaching.

Thought leadership sounds like two big words but in reality, we all are in a position to share powerful insights with our customers.

How? Simple, all salespeople have access to their existing client base, who all have experienced the same challenges. By interacting with them and witnessing various ways in which your clients tackled their problems, you can easily develop insights that would help others.

In addition, by focusing on cause and effect of customer issues you can deepen those insights. By thinking about the bigger picture of what causes typical problems in your industry space (be it operational, financial, social, political or organisational) and the wider (and not so obvious) consequences of these issues, you can structure an insight in a particular way that makes the recipient go *"hmmmmm, that's a thought!"*.

If you are good at public speaking, great, find a platform and get the word out. But to be known as a thought leader is all about sharing insights—therefore, just tweeting powerful nuggets of information or sharing ideas and new ways of thinking via LinkedIn or email can also produce powerful results.

> Remember: Thought leadership is about delivering the answers to the biggest questions on the minds of your current and future customers.

Insight 178

Macrosalesonomics

In school, I used to enjoy studying Economics. However, if I'm honest with myself, I did feel like concepts such as Keynesian vs. Neoclassical models or price elasticity appeared all too theoretical for me. *"How does this affect the person on the street in the real world?"* I would muse to myself. The answer came to me shockingly when I took out a variable rate mortgage, bought my first home and interest rates started to rise...

A Rainmaker sees nothing in isolation. The watchword is *interdependence*: individuals, businesses, organisations and governments co-existing in an interdependent ecosystem that is influenced by both natural events and man-made decisions. Macroeconomics (the behaviour of the economy within a determined region) can have a massive effect on sales performance and even the life expectancy of the company one is part of.

Financial traders make money on the markets (through stocks, derivatives, commodities, foreign exchange, etc.) and whether these go up or down, traders have strategies and tactics to work with the change to their advantage. In fact, the more volatile the market, the more money they can make. This is true with selling. Rainmakers study the effect changes to the wider economy have on their customers and the need to solve their problems. They change strategy when selling in difficult times and change again when selling in easier times. Rainmakers think outside the box and look for opportunities caused by a macroeconomic shift whilst competitors keep on doing what they have always done and hope for the best.

Study the economy in your region; understand the signs and the markers, and innovate how you approach customers, how you help them with their reformed goals or even how you re-profile your customer type due to the change. Innovate.

> # Remember: Understanding the nature of business will keep you in Business.

Insight 179

Microsalesonomics

If Macroeconomics is about the behaviour of the economy as a whole, microeconomics is about the behaviour of *actors* within the economy due to the economy. The actor could be an individual, a company, or even an industry. The average salesperson is completely unaware of how these actors behave in varying circumstances, let alone how to benefit from changes.

Take for example commodity price falls due to the tempered demand in China's slowing economy. Who is affected positively? Consumers (lower prices) and certain companies (cheaper manufacturing costs). What about negatively? Mining companies, oil producers, governments (less tax receipts). What about equity markets? These macro-economic changes offer new opportunities for the enterprising mind which understands how to analyse and interpret these dynamics.

Rainmakers appreciate that you don't have to be an economist to understand cause and effect and to open your eyes to what's happening around you. Rainmakers study their market, their industry, their customer's verticals, their customer's customers, their customer's competitors and use the changes in actor behaviour to create and demonstrate value. Rainmakers know that changes always influence a customer's behaviour and decision-making process.

I know a Rainmaker who sells computer hardware and software

systems. She constantly says, "When times are good, sell on 'nice to have', but when times are difficult, sell on 'must have' like their jobs depended on it". It is a small change in tact and messaging but it worked for her. Now's the time to discover what will work for you.

Remember: Samuel Lover once wrote, "Circumstances are the rulers of the weak; they are but the instruments of the wise".

Insight 180

The Silver Bullet

Yes, there is a silver bullet when it comes to being successful as a Rainmaker. However, a bullet does not act in isolation, so in the spirit of keeping this analogy alive, let us put the silver bullet to one side for a moment and explore where the silver bullet would come from: *the (silver?) gun.*

Relative to what this book has expressed, let us break down the gun into its basic parts.

The Grip: The grip is the part of the gun that you hold. Grasping the gun properly and steadily is paramount for safety as well as for directing the silver bullet to hit its intended target. The grip can represent self-belief, preparation and hard work. Without these things, the silver bullet will travel to the wrong destination.

The Sights: Aiming the gun is critical to hitting the intended target. Both front and rear sights work in tandem to get off a perfect shot. The front sight can represent goal-setting and the rear sight can represent learning from experience, both of which are critical to achieving success as a Rainmaker.

The Trigger: The firing sequence begins with the trigger. If this works properly, the rest of the process is set in motion. The process of prospecting can express this. Without smart, varied and consistent prospecting, nothing really starts. Without a start, you have no pipeline; therefore, you have no business.

The Hammer: This ignites the charge and propels the silver bullet out of the gun. Imagine the hammer as the Rainmaker's deal-making abilities such as building rapport, questioning, structuring the commercials, helping the customer to reach their goal and closing the deal in a win-win fashion.

The Barrel: The tube in which the silver bullet will travel to exit the gun once fired. The pipeline of the Rainmaker can typify this. It **must** be healthy and buoyant at all times.

With all this in place, out comes the *silver bullet.* So from this analogy, what does the silver bullet represent? *Value.* Plain and simple. The silver bullet is being the embodiment of real, demonstrable and dynamic value to the Rainmaker's customers, company and, just as importantly, him or herself.

> # Remember: Value is the Rainmaker's Silver Bullet.

Bonus Insight

"There are moments, Jeeves, when one asks oneself, 'Do trousers matter?'"

The saying goes: *"You never get a second chance to make a first impression"*. In the reality of the corporate selling environment, you do have more than one chance but you would have a lot of catching up to get ahead of your competitor. To be a Rainmaker, one has to act like a Rainmaker, talk like a Rainmaker, reason like a Rainmaker and *dress like a Rainmaker*. First impressions don't count—it's the *right* first impression that counts.

Rainmakers are not there to be the most fashionable-looking people, with slick expensive clothes and jewellery. When it comes to what you wear, the key to the right impression is actually no impression at all. Your attire should not cause any distraction whatsoever from what you are there for. Rainmakers meet prospects to get down to business with impressions and opinions coming from what is being discussed and actioned upon, and not the salesperson's dress sense.

Dress smart and sharp with attention to detail. Dress, however, with a quiet understatement, giving an air of importance but not being ostentatious. A sense of quiet confidence and high self-esteem through your clothing style is the goal.

The key to getting this right is to do your research. On suit types matching body types, on suit/shirt/tie colour combinations, tie knot/shirt collar combinations, hair, makeup, accessories and shoes. The more you understand and develop your own business dress sense, the more successful at getting the client focus immediately on what you have to say and how you say it.

Remember: Clothes don't make the Rainmaker, but neither does a bad dress sense!

Epilogue

Much Ado about Something

If you really want to know the ultimate secret to being a Rainmaker, here it is…

Find out what you love, train yourself to be excellent at it and then offer it to the world and watch your and everybody's lives transform.

Thank you for being part of this journey.

About the Author

Google me ☺.

For more insights sign up at
www.makerain.net

Made in the USA
Charleston, SC
04 January 2017